RUNNING ON RAILS

Railway Heritage

RUNNING ON RAILS

A fascinating journey along Britain's railways old and new

John Legg and Ian Peaty

A Silver Link Book

Silver Link Books
Mortons Media Group Limited
Media Centre
Morton Way
Horncastle
LN9 6JR
Tel/Fax: 01507 529535

email: sohara@mortons.co.uk

Website: www.nostalgiacollection.com

First published in 2020

British Library Cataloguing in Publication Data

A catalogue record for this book is available from the British Library.

Printed and bound in the Czech Republic

ISBN 978 1 85794 548 5

At Deep Duffryn Colliery on the renowned Mountain Ash system is 0-6-0ST No 1, built by Hudswell Clarke, Works No 1885, in 1955. It was rebuilt, but you will note that someone forgot to replace the dome cover! *Adrian Booth*

Contents

Introduction: the revealing landscape

For many of us any railway can provide an enormous source of enjoyment, discussion and photographic opportunities, not just for the enthusiast but for everyone.

Being a commuter by train into one of our cities is just a part of the working day and probably does very little to stir the emotions other than 'It's arrived late again!' But, for those of us who never use the train except for a special occasion it can be exciting, whether it be on Eurostar racing down the high-speed line at 186mph (300km/h) towards the Channel Tunnel or on a preserved line with a train being hauled at 25mph (40km/h) by an elegantly turned out steam locomotive that is 100 years old and still going strong. You smell it, you hear it and it is not difficult to cast your mind back to those times, and it may well stir your emotions.

Over many years of friendship and a shared enthusiasm for transport we, the authors, have taken many unique photographs and, together with photographs from other sources, we would like to share them with you and maybe stir the memories of your younger days; we may also perhaps generate some enthusiasm in those of you who have not looked that closely at the railways you travel on today. We will also look behind the scenes of some important industrial railways that were constructed for the brewing industry, quarrying and general manufacturing, some of which are household names, and for war work, which most people probably did not know existed.

We start this book by giving some background to the last days of the steam locomotive and the introduction of diesel and electric traction, as the forerunners of our modern-day network.

The last days of steam

After the ravages of the Second World War, Europe was forced to undertake a massive rebuilding of its railway infrastructure, including locomotives and rolling stock that had been severely damaged by Allied bombing. This presented the opportunity to phase out steam and renew their networks based on electric and diesel traction. Several countries rapidly made headway in this direction, generating new ideas and advancing railway technology.

In Britain, which had suffered far less damage all round, steam locomotives, many of ancient vintage, were kept going, although every aspect of the network was in need of maintenance or replacement to restore it to its pre-war condition. However, with abundant quantities of quality coal readily available from UK coalfields, the 'Big Four' railway companies persisted with steam locomotion. Even when nationalisation came in 1948, the four British Railways regions were supplied with a thousand of the new Standard designs of steam locomotives. British Railways built 2,537 steam locomotives between 1948 and 1960; the last to be built was *Evening Star*, No 92220, a 2-10-0 freight locomotive designed by R. A. Riddles and built at the old Great Western Railway (GWR) works at Swindon. This 9F locomotive had the honour of hauling the last 'Pines Express' from Manchester to Bournemouth over the iconic Somerset & Dorset Joint Railway (S&DJR) on 8 September 1962, before the service was rerouted.

The inevitable end of steam was accelerated by the 1955 Modernisation Plan, whereby British Railways was to invest in new locomotives and rolling stock, starting with diesel multiple units and ordering 'pilot scheme' main-line diesel locomotives offered by the different manufacturers at that time. This new departure also took into consideration the 'Clean Air Act' and the need to clean up the air we breathe, as steam locomotives were a major source of air pollution.

When Dr Richard Beeching (Chairman of the British Railways Board) was tasked with changing the future of British Railways to make it a modern and profitable organisation, he launched his first report in March 1963, called 'The Reshaping of British Railways'. It recommended that 2,363 stations and 5,000 miles (8,000km) of line be closed owing to heavy economic losses, mainly caused by competition from road transport and family cars that had become the favoured means of transport for going on holiday in the UK. On a positive note, Dr Beeching recommended that freight should be containerised and modern high-capacity freight wagons built. Freight services should concentrate on oil, minerals and 'merry-go-round' coal trains for the power stations that generated the country's electricity. But by then nuclear, oil and gas power stations were coming on stream to supply most of the nation's electricity, further reducing the need for coal, resulting in the closure of many coal mines. Much of the track closures were due to duplication of the former private companies' routes in many areas, chiefly in the south Wales coalfield, the Midlands, the North East and Devon and Cornwall, where the two counties would find themselves virtually without railway access. These facts were emphasised by Dr Beeching in his second report of 16 February 1965, 'The Development of Major Trunk Routes'.

Left: A Hunslet 0-6-0ST, Works No 3840 built in 1956 and named *Pamela*, reverses coal wagons past the weighbridge cabin at Maesteg Washery in May 1972. After dieselisation the loco was retained as 'spare engine'. *Adrian Booth*

At an unknown location, circa 1960, is Type 2 Bo-Bo diesel-electric locomotive No D6135, built in 1959 by the North British Locomotive Co of Glasgow with a MAN 12-cylinder diesel engine producing 1,100bhp. Another unidentified Type 2 is resting on the same track a short distance behind.

During the 1960s the introduction of diesels for all types of work continued, with steam locomotives being withdrawn and consigned to the scrap heap. A total of 17 British Railways workshops took in hundreds of locomotives, stored and rusting on sidings awaiting the cutter's torch. Two of the largest privately owned scrap yards belonged to Woodham Brothers and T. W. Ward.

Not everything was converted to diesel at that time, as there was the existing Southern Region 750V DC third-rail London commuter network; although ageing, it was, even then, a congested and complex arrangement that was ripe for expansion and modernisation to meet the growing needs of the London rush hour public from South London, Kent, Sussex and Hampshire.

On the Southern Region the last steam-hauled trains ran on 9 July 1967 and included the last boat train to Southampton Docks, which was hauled by 'West Country' 'Pacific' *Clovelly*, and the 'Channel Islands Boat Express', hauled by 'Merchant Navy' *Holland-Afrika Line*. These

luxurious Pullman trains had now gone forever.

On 11 August 1968 the last BR steam-hauled train in Britain, the 'Fifteen Guinea Special', ran from Liverpool to Manchester via Carlisle, with each of four steam locomotives taking the reins at each stage. The price of £15s 15d was highly inflated because of the vast number of people wanting to take the train. A complete ban on steam came into force on 12 August.

Fortunately, as steam locomotives were being scrapped the National Railway Museum, now based in York, rescued a variety from all regions for the National Collection, and many of these are now running on preserved railway lines.

After three steamless years British Rail relented and in 1971 allowed special, steam-hauled trains to run on the UK network.

As branch and minor lines closed, the preservation movement was getting itself organised to buy stretches of line and reopen them to run trains for themselves and for the enjoyment of the public. Many rusting

This is the same location with another Type 2 Bo-Bo diesel electric locomotive, No D5032, built by BR in 1958 with a 1,160bhp six-cylinder Sulzer engine. There is still steam activity in the background.

This 0-6-0T locomotive No 30072, seen here at Guildford shed, was built for the United States Transport Corps at the Vulcan works in Pennsylvania in 1943. It saw brief service on the continent after the Second World War and was one of a batch of 14 bought by the Southern Railway (SR) in 1947. They initially worked within Southampton Docks.

locomotives were rescued from the scrap yards and lovingly rebuilt by the capable hands of the dedicated enthusiasts. The first standard-gauge railway to re-open was the Bluebell Railway in West Sussex, which ran its first train on 7 August 1960. Some years earlier, the first narrow-gauge railway in preservation was the Talyllyn in Mid-Wales, which reopened in 1951. It was a run-down slate railway running from Towyn Wharf station on the coast to Abergynolwyn up in the wooded hills, and became the world's first heritage railway. There are now many standard- and narrow-gauge steam locomotives operating on preserved lines around the UK to the delight of both enthusiasts and the general public. All was not lost!

This 2-6-4T locomotive, No 42616 of LMS Stanier design, was built by North British at Glasgow in 1937 and withdrawn from service in 1967. It is seen here at Kings Langley station, Hertfordshire, in the early 1960s en route to Euston with a commuter train.

A very dirty 'Q1' 0-6-0 Second World War 'Austerity' locomotive, No 33040, is seen at Nine Elms shed in the early 1960s. Designed by Bulleid for the Southern Railway, it was a lighter-weight locomotive than the 'Merchant Navy' Class that it resembled and could access 97% of SR lines. No 33040 was the last 'Q1', having been built in 1942 at Ashford Works in Kent. They were said to be the ugliest locos in service!

A number of locos taken out of service in the late 1960s, which were eventually going to a scrap yard, are seen here at Normanton Yard, West Yorkshire. On the left is a Hughes-designed 2-6-0 tender loco, No 42902, known as a 'Crab', built at Crewe in 1930 and withdrawn in 1964. In the middle is No 40181, a Stanier Class 3P-B 2-6-2T built at Derby Works in 1938 and withdrawn in 1962. On the right is a 2-6-0 4F-A of Ivatt design, built in 1951 and withdrawn from service in 1963.

Left: At Old Oak depot, looking reasonably turned out, is Collett 4-6-0 No 7032 *Denbigh Castle*, built at the former GWR's Swindon Works in 1950 and withdrawn from service in 1964.

Right: GWR Class '2251' 0-6-0 tender loco No 2218 is in Salisbury yard. It was built at the GWR's Swindon Works in 1940 and withdrawn in 1964. Its last shed was Templecombe in Somerset.

Below: This somewhat dismal view shows an unidentified yard of grimy locomotives probably getting steam up for a day's work in the late 1950s. It is difficult to identify most except for the two in the foreground being Standard 2MT 2-6-0s designed by R. A. Riddles and built at BR Darlington Works between 1952 and 1956.

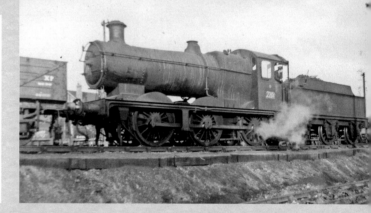

Life after Steam

The need for vast quantities of coal reduced, as it was not required by steam locomotives, and increasing numbers of power stations were no longer reliant on coal, resulting in a dramatic decline in the income from that part of BR's freight business.

Following Dr Beeching's recommendations, the rail industry was forced to find freight business that would replace the income lost from the many coal trains that would normally trundle from the collieries on a daily basis. At the same time the outdated mixed freight trains

Class 66 No 66018 hauls a rake of flat wagons loaded with rail for Network Rail, seen here at Swinton, South Yorkshire, in 2016. *Adrian Booth*

that carried everything from small parcels and perishables to industrial machinery all in one train soon became a distant memory. Freight was now being hauled by diesel locomotives, and was made up of block trains of just containers, tankers or large steel wagons loaded with sand and stone in its various forms from the many quarries around the country. These natural minerals continue to be increasingly transported by rail.

The passenger side of BR continued, with trains now hauled by a variety of diesel locomotives. However, in line with Dr Beeching's report to modernise the railway network, in 1960 BR introduced the Blue Pullman diesel-electric multiple units, as a fast and efficient alternative to the ever-increasing popularity of road transport. They ran from London St Pancras to Manchester Central and from Paddington to Bristol. They were reasonably successful, but were eventually withdrawn in 1973, paving the way for the Intercity 125 that has been with us since 1975.

Passing Rotherham football ground in 2014 is Class 66 No 66154 with wagons loaded with steel products. *Adrian Booth*

A coal train headed by Class 66 No 66403 waits at a red signal approaching Northorpe level crossing en route from Immingham Docks to Eggborough Power Station in North Yorkshire. The photograph was taken on a cold and snow-covered winter's day, 21 December 2010. *Mark Wyard*

'Heathrow Express' Class 332 EMU No 33201 stands at Paddington Station in 2016. Siemens built 14 sets of four- and five-car units that were introduced in 1997 and powered through pantograph collection from a 25kV overhead catenary system.

A Class 395 Hitachi 'Javelin' EMU is seen here at Canterbury East. They have dual power systems to enable them to run on both the 25kV catenary system of the High Speed (HS1) line in Kent to St Pancras, and on the Southeastern 750V third-rail network. They were introduced in 2009 and have proved to be reliable and efficient.

1. London

London, of course, is the main transport hub of the UK and over the past 30 years much has been achieved in providing a more efficient and comfortable experience for the daily commuter and longer-distance traveller, especially on the railways.

London's newest commercial and financial centre at Canary Wharf in Docklands is now easily accessible from the City by the Docklands Light Railway, while the massive Crossrail project, now named the Elizabeth Line, is nearing completion and will provide fast access from the suburbs in the east and the west of London with new subterranean interchanges with major underground and main-line stations. Transport for London continues to improve the Underground and Overground experience for its passengers.

Virtually all railway rolling stock has been replaced, with more careful thought applied to seating arrangements, comfort, onboard toilets, constantly updating digital destination panels, recorded digital voice updates of stations stops, and security cameras. Long-distance travel is now faster, quieter and more comfortable with Wi-Fi and power points, etc.

Stations must not be forgotten, as over the years many underground stations have being remodelled or brought up to date, and the London termini have been miraculously transformed into beautiful structures while maintaining their heritage from the steam era.

Some very significant and well-known industries such as the Ford Motor Company and Guinness also one operated railways in the London area with their own internal systems, which connected with the national network.

During 2010 the York Theatre Royal in association with the National Railway Museum staged E. Nesbit's *The Railway Children* in the disused International Station at Waterloo. Eurostar trains were now terminating at the rebuilt International station at St Pancras. Great Northern 'G' Class 4-2-2 'Stirling Single' No 1, built in 1870 in the company's Doncaster Works with 8ft 1in (2.46m) driving wheels, was a star of the show.

London termini

Most major railway routes today emanate from London to reach a variety of towns and cities in the north, east, south and west of the country, including Wales and Scotland. London can boast 12 termini, most of which were opened around the 1840s during the time of the 'railway mania', when competitive railway companies were fighting for the most lucrative routes and places to build their termini. The companies coming in from the south side of the River Thames were forced to build bridges over the river to the north bank, so that their passengers could alight at their place of work in the City of London or the West End. These were, of course, the days of smoky steam locomotives, very basic carriage stock, mostly made of wood with minimal gas lighting and no toilets.

Today these stations are teeming with millions of long-distance travellers, commuters and day trippers benefiting from modern electric and diesel units that are fast, clean and comfortable with onboard toilets.

This unusual view of the undercroft of St Pancras station during the 1950s shows the storage facilities for barrels of beer that came down from Burton-on-Trent in the Midlands where many of the major brewers were situated. Since the rebuilding and reopening of St Pancras in 2007, the undercroft has been converted into a plethora of restaurants, gift shops and newsagents.

The following are the termini in order of opening, with broadly the areas served by each:

Euston   **1837**
  West Coast Main Line to Birmingham, the Midlands, Glasgow and Edinburgh
Fenchurch Street   **1841**
  East London, Essex to Southend Central
Waterloo   **1848**
  South-west to Exeter and Weymouth, Surrey, Hampshire and Berkshire
King's Cross   **1852**
  East Coast Main Line to Glasgow and Edinburgh, regional trains to Norfolk, Cambridgeshire and Hertfordshire
Paddington   **1854**
  Services west to Reading, Bristol, South Wales and Heathrow Airport
Victoria 1860
  South-east London, Kent, Sussex and Surrey, and Gatwick Airport
Charing Cross   **1864**
  South London, Kent & East Sussex
Cannon Street   **1866**
  South London

King's Cross station was originally opened in 1852 for the Great Northern Railway and has a truly impressive facade. By 2013 restoration work was completed, making it fit for the 21st century with more space, new entrances and better facilities. The interior is modern and impressive.

St Pancras   **1868**
The Midlands – Leicester, Derby and Sheffield and HS1 line for fast local services to Kent and Eurostar services to Paris and Brussels via the Channel Tunnel

Liverpool Street   **1874**
Hertfordshire, east London, Essex to Southend Victoria, Suffolk, Norfolk and Stansted Airport

Marylebone   **1899**
Oxford, Birmingham and local services to Buckinghamshire

London Bridge   **1900**
Through services from Charing Cross, south-west London and Sussex

The broad areas served by these stations have some interesting passenger and industrial stories to tell from both past and present.

Left: In King's Cross station are Virgin Trains diesel-electric Class 43 HST No 43208 and a Grand Central five-car Class 180 'Adelante' DMU. The Virgin train is being cleaned in readiness for its trip back up the East Coast Main Line to Edinburgh, while the Grand Central will take the East Coast Main Line to Sunderland.

Below: This view inside King's Cross station shows how well our splendid termini can be modernised and the existing buildings integrated. The roofing, lighting and the shops greatly improve the travellers' experience. The restoration plan was completed in 2012.

Above left: This view of the busy concourse at Liverpool Street station was taken during a winter evening in 2015. While the original building survives, built by the Great Eastern Railway in 1874, recent changes have introduced modern facilities to make the commuter's life a more pleasant one.

The facade of Marylebone station has a very pleasant provincial look about it. It was built by the Great Central Railway and opened in 1899. Although, for a terminus, it has only six platforms, it is always busy with Chiltern Railways commuter services to Aylesbury and High Wycombe and main-line services to Birmingham.

Just about to leave Marylebone is a Chiltern Railways train destined for Birmingham Moor Street. It is headed by Direct Rail Services (DRS) diesel-electric Class 68 No 68008 *Avenger*, built by Vossloh-Spain in 2014.

Class 43 HST No 43192 has just arrived at Paddington station in 2015. Class 43s are now being phased out for new BR Class 802 bi-mode (diesel/25kV AC) units manufactured by Hitachi. Paddington was designed by Isambard Kingdom Brunel and opened in 1854 for his Great Western Railway to Bristol.

Above: A broad view of activity at Paddington station shows 'Heathrow Express' Class 332 No 332005 on the right, Class 166 No 166216 in GWR dark green livery to its left, and Class 43 No 40070. There are two other unidentified Class 43s beyond.

Above: East Midlands Class 222 DMU No 222012 is soon to depart from St Pancras for Nottingham on the Midland Main Line. These DMUs, capable of 125mph (200km/h), were built by Bombardier at its Bruges (Belgium) plant and introduced in 2004. They have recently been completely refurbished.

Left: Here is the unmistakable statue by Martin Jennings of John Betjeman looking up appreciatively at the fine roof of St Pancras. Betjeman, Jane Hughes Fawcett and the Victorian Society led a hard campaign to save the station and hotel from demolition and were rewarded for their work in 1967 when it was given Grade 1 listing.

Located at the end of Victoria Street in Belgravia, Victoria station was built as a joint venture to enable the LB&SCR and LC&DR to terminate their trains on the north side of the Thames. The current station is in two halves, which accommodated the SE&CR (an amalgamation of the SER and the LC&DR) on the left side and the LB&SCR on the right, and includes the Grosvenor Hotel. Both new parts of the station were opened around 1908.

Two Class 375 EMUs, Nos 603 and 605, in Southeastern blue livery, are about to depart from Victoria's Platforms 3 and 4 for the Medway towns, Dover and Ramsgate on the North Kent Line, and Ashford and Canterbury West via Maidstone East on the Mid Kent Line. The units were built by Bombardier at its Derby Works from 1999 and obtain power from the 700V DC third-rail system.

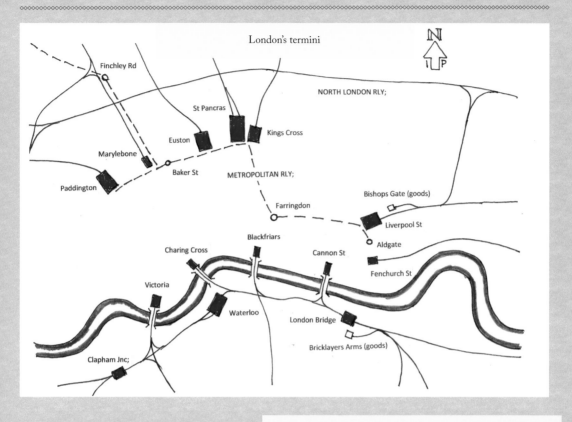

London's termini

Finchley Rd

NORTH LONDON RLY;

St Pancras

Euston

Kings Cross

Marylebone

Baker St

METROPOLITAN RLY;

Paddington

Farringdon

Bishops Gate (goods)

Liverpool St

Aldgate

Blackfriars

Charing Cross

Cannon St

Fenchurch St

Victoria

Waterloo

London Bridge

Bricklayers Arms (goods)

Clapham Jnc;

The Midland Railway's St Pancras station.

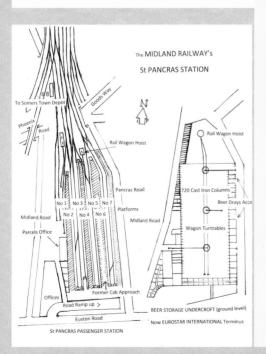

The MIDLAND RAILWAY's
St PANCRAS STATION

To Somers Town Depot

Goods Way

Phoenix Road

Rail Wagon Hoist

Rail Wagon Hoist

Pancras Road

720 Cast Iron Columns

Beer Drays Acce

No 1 No 3 No 5 No 7
No 2 No 4 No 6

Platforms

Midland Road

Midland Road

Wagon Turntables

Parcels Office

Offices

Former Cab Approach

Road Ramp up

Euston Road

BEER STORAGE UNDERCROFT (ground level)

Now EUROSTAR INTERNATIONAL Terminus

ST PANCRAS PASSENGER STATION

Famous trains from London's termini

Paintings by Ian Peaty

King's Cross: The LNER's *Silver Link* and its matching silver coaches forming the 'Silver Jubilee' train on the East Coast route.

Flying Scotsman in its original condition in full flight in Scotland with a train of LNER teak coaches.

Above: LNER No 10000, the only British locomotive of the 4-6-4 wheel arrangement, designed by Gresley in 1929, and rebuilt as an 'A4' Class 'Pacific' in 1935.

Above right: Liverpool Street: LNER Class 'B2' No 1671 *Royal Sovereign*, running from Liverpool Street to Ipswich, is seen here on Belstead Bank in 1937.

Right: Euston: The LMS's 'Coronation Scot' ran between London and Glasgow in 6½ hours on 5 July 1937. Five locos, Nos 6220-24, were built specially for this service.

Right: A 'Princess Coronation' 'Pacific', pride of the LMS, with its matching red coaches – a majestic sight.

Below left: Paddington: A GWR 'Castle' Class locomotive leaves Twerton Tunnel, east of Bath, on its journey east towards the capital.

Below right: Waterloo: An ex-LSWR Class 'K10' 4-4-0, built in 1901 to a design of Dugald Drummond, is seen in Southern Railway days – a locomotive of true elegance.

The Southern Railway's international pride, the 'Golden Arrow', heads towards France hauled by a streamlined 'Merchant Navy' Class 'Pacific'.

London's Underground

All of London's termini have access to the London Underground network, with eight conveniently located on the Circle Line.

The Metropolitan Line

The world's first underground railway was the Metropolitan, a standard-gauge passenger and freight railway known as the 'Met'. It was built in 1860 and constructed largely by the 'cut and cover' method, whereby the line was built in shallow cuttings beneath existing roads, then covered over.

The Met's first section of line was from Paddington in the west to King's Cross (both major main-line termini), then followed the culverted River Fleet in an open cutting to the new meat market of Smithfield, a mere 3.75 miles (6km), which was opened on 10 January 1863. The trains were steam-hauled and the coaches were wooden with gas lighting. On the first day of opening 38,000 passengers were carried, and in the first year of operation 9.5 million passenger journeys were made. Clearly the concept of connecting main-line stations was a very prudent decision, as it brought people to their workplaces in the City.

Before the Met opened for business in 1863 trials took place to find ways of reducing the amount of smoke and steam that belched from locomotives, as the atmosphere in the tunnels was very unpleasant. The answer was to use a locomotive with steam condensing capabilities. The passenger services

Metropolitan Railway Class 'A' 4-4-0T No 27 was built by Beyer Peacock in Manchester around 1868. These engines were specifically built to condense the steam and burn coke to cut down on the sooty smoke. The large and rather ugly condensing pipe can be seen running across the top of the boiler and down into the cylinder. Note the crew's spectacle plate.

started with broad-gauge GWR condensing 2-4-0T locomotives, then progressed to standard-gauge GNR locomotives. The Met then ordered 18 4-4-0T locomotives from Beyer Peacock of Manchester, and by 1870 a total of 40 had been built. The Met also experimented with smoke reduction and eventually settled for Welsh smokeless coal. As more trains were needed the Met ordered another 24 4-4-0T locomotives of updated design. All these locomotives had a very distinctive appearance with the additional large pipes and vents. At this stage the locomotives did not have driving cabs, but had simple spectacle plates (shield) with a porthole window on either

Baker Street station's façade has hardly changed over the last 156 years since 1863 and is situated at the junction of Marylebone Road and Baker Street (of Sherlock Holmes fame). It has 10 platforms serving both high-level and low-level lines – the Metropolitan, Circle, Hammersmith & City, Bakerloo and Jubilee lines.

side for the driver and fireman; cabs were not fitted until 1895. The District Railway and the Metropolitan agreed to complete an inner Circle Line, which was opened in 1884 and connects with six of the London termini.

However, a solution to the overall pollution problem in the central London tunnels had to be found and the decision was made to electrify the lines. It was decided to use a 600V DC system employing four rails: two running rails, a central conductor rail at -210V and an outside rail at +420V, resulting in a potential difference of 630V DC. To achieve this, the Met built its own coal-fired power station at Neasden in 1904, which supplied five substations with 11kV at 33.3Hz. This was then converted down to 600V DC using rotary converters. The first electric trains ran on 1 January 1905 between Baker Street and Harrow, and on inner London lines by 24 September 1905, with the last steam passenger trains on 23 September 1905. Electrification rendered many steam locomotives redundant, resulting in them being scrapped or sold. This system of electrification is now used across all London's underground network.

Since then the Met has extended its routes in both directions, to Aldgate in the east of the City and west to Amersham and Chesham in Buckinghamshire, Watford in Hertfordshire, and Uxbridge in the London Borough of Hillingdon, with electrification being completed in 1961.

During the years between the 1920s and 1933 the Met was developing land for housing estates and successfully marketing it under the 'Metro-land' brand. Some of the land already belonged to the Met, ostensibly for railway purposes. An estates company was formed, called the Metropolitan Railway Country Estates Ltd, which developed estates near Neasden, Wembley Park, Cecil Park, Pinner, Rickmansworth and Harrow. The Metro-land Guide issued annually by the company's marketing department extolled the virtues of living in the countryside and commuting easily into London. This was ideal commuting country, most apparent when travelling out towards Moor Park, Rickmansworth, Chorley Wood, Chalfont & Latimer and Amersham into 'The good air of the Chilterns'.

The Met had always been a private company, but on 1 July 1933 the London Passenger Transport Board (LPTB) was created as a public corporation and the Met, together with all the other underground railways (the 'tubes'), tram and bus operators, was amalgamated into this giant organisation. A period of rationalisation then followed. The LPTB eventually became London Transport and is now Transport for London.

After the Met was amalgamated into the LPTB in 1933 the Metro-land brand disappeared overnight and the Met became just another part of the London underground network.

The 'tube'

From the 1890s onwards London's Underground network involved the construction of deep-level 11ft 8¼in (Central Line) circular tunnels, hence the name 'tube', bored deep under the City with subterranean stations, escalators and lifts to take the passengers from ground level to their required platforms.

Baker Street's Circle and Hammersmith & City 1863-built platforms are still in use today and were restored to their original design in 1983 with a brick barrel roof and replica electric lighting.

The first tube to open was the City & South London Railway in 1890, which ran from Stockwell in South London to King William Street in the City; the tube tunnel was bored under the River Thames and now forms a part of the Northern Line. The second, in 1899, was the Waterloo & City Line, running from Waterloo station, under the Thames to Bank station in the City; it remains that way today, lovingly called 'the drain'. All trains were hauled by an electric locomotive until replaced by electric multiple units of the type we see today.

The Central London Railway (now the Central Line) opened in 1900 between Bank and Shepherds Bush in the west. This eventually extended further west to West Ruislip and Ealing Broadway, and east to Epping in Essex, with a loop from Leytonstone to Hainault and round to Woodford. It serves 49 stations over 46 miles (74km) and is the busiest line on the network, carrying around 260 million passengers a year, and rising. It is probably true to say that it serves the most important areas of London – the City and the West End – running directly under Oxford Street. In 1957 the original 6½-mile (10.5km) Great Eastern Railway line from Epping to Ongar, which was steam-hauled using GER Class

Parts of the high-level areas where trains run still have the original Metropolitan brown, blue and cream tiles from 1863. This view also shows the iconic Transport for London roundel, which has been copied in various parts of the world, especially India.

Above: This is *Sarah Siddons*, one of 20 electric Bo-Bo locomotives built by Metropolitan-Vickers for the Metropolitan Railway in 1923 for its Baker Street, Amersham and Aylesbury route. Capable of reaching 60mph (96km/h), power was taken from the normal four-rail 600V DC network. This engine was retired in 1962, but is preserved and makes the occasional trip for enthusiasts, etc.
Oxyman, Wikimedia Commons

Right: One of the latest S8 ('S' is sub-surface) stock trains introduced on the Metropolitan Line from 2010 for services on the Baker Street to Amersham route is seen here about to depart from Baker Street. The units are manufactured by Bombardier in Derby and include air-conditioning, fully motorised axles and regenerative braking. The line voltage has been increased from 630V DC to 750V DC to accommodate the extra power requirement.

Right: A westbound train of 1923 stock approaches Loughton station on the Central Line in the winter of 1961, a year before the replacement 1962 stock was introduced. This photo was taken by one of the authors with a third-hand Ensign Ful-Vue camera using 120 roll film and a shutter speed of 1/30th second; the printed photo size was 6cm by 6cm.

Below right: Metro-Cammell placed this advertisement in one of the transport magazines of the day to announce that it had already manufactured 769 cars of the 1,039 cars of the 1962 stock required for the Central and Piccadilly lines. These trains were left in their aluminium finish, came into service in 1962 and ran successfully until February 1995, when the last trains were withdrawn to be replaced by the 1992 stock.

Bottom: The current tube stock on the Central Line is the 1992 stock built by British Rail Engineering and Bombardier and introduced from April 1993. It has many refinements over previous stock, including Automatic Train Operation (ATO) and Automatic Train Protection (ATP), which means that the train can effectively drive itself. They also have Digital Voice Announcement (DVA) for every station along the line.
Tom Page, London, Wikimedia Commons

COMPLETED!

769 **METRO-CAMMELL**

TUBE CARS

FOR **LONDON TRANSPORT**

PICCADILLY AND CENTRAL LINES

Production is in full swing at Metro-Cammell's Midland Works on the second Contract for Tube Cars for London Transport Executive. Two contracts, running concurrently, provide for a total of 1,039 cars for the Piccadilly and Central Lines.

METROPOLITAN-CAMMELL CARRIAGE & WAGON CO. LTD.

HEAD OFFICE: SALTLEY, BIRMINGHAM 8.
LONDON OFFICE: VICARS HOUSE, BROADWAY, WESTMINSTER, S.W.1.

'G69' 2-4-2T locomotives built at Stratford Works in 1904, finally ceased steam operation and became an electrified Central Line branch service through the Essex countryside, stopping at North Weald, Blake Hall and terminating at Ongar. The line finally proved uneconomical and was closed in 1994, but is now the domain of the Epping & Ongar heritage railway.

Most tube trains 'pop out' of their tunnels at some point and travel above ground, especially at the extremities of their lines. All tube trains are standard gauge, are much smaller than their standard railway counterparts and use the four-rail electric traction system of 630V DC. Above all safety is paramount, and all tube line tunnels are continually cleaned and the network updated.

Left: Seen at North Weald station in May 2012 is GWR 0-6-0 pannier tank locomotive No 6430, built at Swindon Works in 1937. It spent a number of years working in the South Wales valleys.

Below: Just passing Blake Hall station, which closed in 1981, is 4-6-0 'Hall' Class *Pitchford Hall*, built at Swindon Works in 1929, hauling a train from Ongar to North Weald.

Epping & Ongar Railway

Although this Great Eastern Railway branch line, opened in 1865, is not strictly 'London', it became a part of London Transport (LT), but was operated by British Rail auto-trains that could access the BR network via the Central Line at Temple Mills, Leyton. The steam auto-trains ran from the eastern end of the Central Line at Epping to Ongar, a distance of 6½ miles (10km) with rural stations at North Weald, Blake Hall (closed in 1981) and Ongar Town.

The single line was finally electrified in 1957, and a shuttle service continued between Epping and Ongar using LT tube stock. Trains were limited to four cars because of the short platforms and low power, as LT would not build a much-needed sub-station. Unfortunately, the line lost money from the start and was closed to passengers in 1994.

The good news is that the line was sold

Right: This old photograph taken in the early 1950s at Epping station shows the auto-train from Ongar headed by an ex-GER 'F5' Holden 2-4-2T steam locomotive built at Stratford Works around 1915.
Ben Brooksbank

Below: A Metro-Cammell tube set of 1962 stock arrives at Ongar prior to the line's closure in 1994. Ongar had become a good place to live and commute to London via Epping. This looks like an evening train arriving during the summer months.

The London Underground station signs are famous the world over, and Ongar has managed to keep them. Over the years these signs are known to be friendly but authoritative in appearance, becoming familiar and reassuring to the travelling public.

to private owners in 1998, and in 2004 the Epping Ongar Railway Preservation Society commenced a DMU service between Ongar and North Weald, which was then extended to Coopersale (near Epping), although there was no platform for passengers to join or leave the train. In January 2007 the line was temporarily closed to enable necessary maintenance to infrastructure, rolling stock and track.

Then in 2007 the railway was sold to a new private owner, who was committed to bringing steam locomotives back to the branch line, but that involved major track work, run-round loops, full signalling and, of course, water.

The Epping & Ongar Railway was then finally reopened on 24 May 2012 running steam and diesel services.

It is hoped to reopen the short stretch of line to Epping Glade, which, although not Epping Town Underground station, is in close proximity.

Right: In 1951 the Festival of Britain was held on the south bank of the River Thames. Rowland Emmet, the renowned cartoonist, designed these wonderfully crazy locomotives and settings as a garden railway in Battersea Park. This is *Neptune* at the station.

Below: This is *Nellie* in full flight through Battersea Park taking her passengers on a 'flight of fancy'.

Below tight: Here *Wild Goose* is ready for the off on her 'Air Service'. This railway was just one of the memorable attractions at the Festival of Britain, and certainly one of the most amusing ones.

Far Tottering & Oystercreek Railway

In 1951 the public enjoyed their first narrow-gauge railway trip in London. There have been other smaller-gauge railways such as the Post Office underground railway and several construction site railways, but none open to the public

This 'public only' use of narrow-gauge track was exceptional in many ways, as its title suggests. The Far Tottering & Oystercreek Railway (FT&OR) was conceived by that eccentric cartoon artist, Rowland Emett, who since the 1940s had regularly contributed to *Punch* magazine. His superb and quirky depiction of a rural British branch-line railway appealed to the British sense of humour. The line was one-third of a mile (0.5 km) long and

was laid to a gauge of 15 inches (381mm). There were three 'steam' locomotives named *Nellie*, *Neptune* and *Wild Goose*, built by Harry Barlow using what was then war surplus material including Fordson diesel engines. And where, might you ask, was this crazy and humorous railway? It was a major attraction at the 1951 Festival of Britain, built on the south bank of the Thames at Lambeth. Opening in May of that year the little railway carried more than two million passengers until 1953, when it was relocated until 1975. The entire exhibition site, included the Dome of Discovery, the slender silver 'Skylon', the Transport Pavilion and many other scientific attractions were all demolished when the exhibition closed with the exception of the iconic Royal Festival Concert Hall.

The aim of the festival was to give the public 'A Tonic for the Nation' after the Second World War, and this it certainly did. The nation had suffered extreme hardships during the five years of war and its aftermath, and the Festival of Britain raised the spirits and aspirations of the country. The exhibition was to show the nation and the world that we could become the world's music scene and fashion industry supreme, not forgetting engineering, architecture and design of everything that was coming into the modern world. It was no coincidence that the festival was held almost 100 years to the day since the Great Exhibition of 1851 at the Crystal Palace. In the 1951 exhibition a 'Britannia' Class 'Pacific', No 70004 *William Shakespeare*, was put on display from 4 May until September. She had been built at Crewe in March of that year and was turned

out in a 'special exhibition finish' – just superb.

The railway site had previously been Victorian industrial buildings and railway sidings, and after the exhibition the site was cleared and returned to nature as Battersea Park Gardens. The only exception to remain in use is the Royal Festival Concert Hall.

The FT&OR had run-round loops at each end with non-working semaphore signals and crane in Emett's inimitable style. Coaches were both open-sided and some with ornate canopies, all painted in a delightful range of pastel colours – not your normal railway company livery!

Fortunately Birmingham City Museum has several of Emett's creations on public display, which reveal his wonderful eccentricity of design. Sadly the three locomotives of the Far Tottering & Oystercreek Railway have finally hit the buffer stops.

Guinness Park Royal Brewery

The Guinness company was founded in Dublin in 1759 at St James's Gate by Arthur Guinness at the age of 31. The growing 'stout' business necessitated a 1ft 10in (558mm) gauge internal railway system for the movement of malt and hops and coal for the boilers, and for moving the casks of beer within the premises. Unlike most

other brewers, Guinness did not own any public houses.

Guinness benefitted from other brewers who were reducing their own dark beers such as porter, which generally remained very popular, especially in London. Guinness was bulk shipped in the company's own vessels from Dublin to London, where bottling was carried out by those brewers and other agents, resulting

The two 'Planet' locomotives were built locally by F. C. Hibberd & Co Ltd. At the front is *Carpenter* (works No 3270) built December 1948, then *Walrus* (Works No 3271) built February 1949; they are seen here at the reception sidings in June 1985. Note that *Carpenter* displays the 'golden harp' logo, but *Walrus* does not.

in complex distribution network to pubs and off-licences, etc.

The market for stout was constantly growing in the UK, which prompted the directors to approve building on a new 'greenfield' site in north-west London at Park Royal in the 1930s. The site selected was close to the newly constructed North Circular Road and adjacent to the GWR goods line. The architect was Sir Gilbert Scott, who designed an Art Deco building similar to several other period properties in the area, and it opened with the first brew on 21 February 1936. The site comprised 137 acres, and became integral with London's largest industrial estate. A connection was made to the GWR, a standard-gauge track curving sharply into the eastern boundary with six reception sidings each capable of holding 45 of the old 12- or

Two ex-BR Class 08 diesels, *Lion* and *Unicorn*, replaced the 'Planets' in July 1985. Both were liveried in the Guinness black, red and gold colours and used for shunting around the yard. Interestingly, the 'golden harp' on the side of one loco is on the fourth panel and on the other the fifth panel – a painter's error?

A long view of the reception sidings shows the two 'Planet' locomotives waiting for their next assignment.

15-ton wagons. An overhead gantry permitted the loading and unloading of 41-barrel capacity (1,476 gallons or 6,710 litres) circular tanks for distribution to the Channel Islands and the Isle of Man. Three other sidings diverged westward to serve the malt and hop stores, and one ran into the boiler house for coal and removal of ashes. In-house locomotives were provided by a Sentinel 0-4-0, No 13, then a pannier tank 0-6-0 of Class '1901' as well as Class '2021s' and '57xxs'. A locomotive shed was eventually erected in 1948 to house two new diesel locomotives

These two 'Planet' 0-4-0 diesel-mechanical locos, named *Walrus* (Works No 3317) and *Carpenter* (Works No 3270) were built in 1948 by F. C. Hibberd & Co Ltd, neighbours to Guinness at Park Royal. They had 144hp Paxman engines with Westinghouse brake systems, and were painted in dark blue with coach lining and gold 'harp' logos, while the buffer beams and wheels were in scarlet red. In 1985 the pair were retired and were replaced by two ex-BR Class 08 0-6-0s, appropriately named *Lion* and *Unicorn*. Their life at Park Royal was terminated in 1995 when the inevitable road transport took over. Guinness Park Royal was the last UK brewery to install a rail system and also the last operational private system. Today the limited sidings are utilised as a 'virtual quarry' for aggregate distribution.

Above: The Class 08 shunters were renamed *Carpenter* and *Walrus* after the original 'Planets'. *Carpenter* is seen here shunting bogie vans on the malt intake sidings.

Right: This picture taken in the early 1950s shows *Carpenter* shunting a six-wheel flat wagon with a securely chained-down road tanker trailer wagon. The BR 14-ton flat wagon has 'Return to Park Royal' painted on the side. The tanker was made by R. A. Dyson of Liverpool with a glass-lined inner tank.

Willesden Junction

This renowned and complex junction is located at Harlesden in north-west London on the West Coast Main Line from Euston. A station to replace the original London & Birmingham Railway facility was constructed by the London & North Western Railway (LNWR) and opened on 1 September, 1866, with two platforms.

During 1869 a high-level crossing was built at right angles to the main line by the North London Railway with its own platforms and pedestrian access to the LNWR platforms below, which became known as the low-level station. In 1910 two bay platforms were added facing London, together with two outer fast tracks.

The LNWR built a large locomotive depot on the south side of the line to the west of the station in 1879, then the LMS opened an additional roundhouse in 1929; these closed in 1965 with the demise of steam and the area is now a Freightliner Depot.

Willesden Junction's original two low-level platforms were removed when the main line was electrified and the curves eased in 1962. Today the West Coast Main Line passes through and the station serves the London Overground and the Bakerloo Line tube. The high-level lines see much freight traffic from north London and at the lower level a branch curves to the south towards Acton and the major Hanson aggregates depot alongside the former GWR main line to the west from Paddington.

On the other side of the main line Willesden Traction Maintenance Depot (TMD) provides maintenance for both EMUs and DMUs for London Overground, Chiltern Railways, London Midland and

Above: This view shows both low- and high-level stations with the electrified West Coast Main Line from Euston station on the left. The island platform (Platforms 1, 2 and 3) serves the 750V DC line for the London Overground Euston-Watford Junction service, with a Class 378 EMU just leaving, as well as the Bakerloo Underground service between Harrow & Wealdstone and Elephant & Castle. Beyond is the high-level station (Platforms 4 and 5) for the North and West London lines.

Above: This West Coast train headed by Class 86 No 86213 *Lancashire Witch* is being hauled by a Class 66 towards Euston. This is not unusual when a diversion onto a non-electrified line is required. The former main-line low-level platforms were in the open space to the right, and lines on the extreme right connect with the GWR at Acton and thence south to the Southern Railway. On the extreme left is the Traction Maintenance Depot.

Right: A Southern bi-mode Class 377 EMU is travelling north towards Watford Junction and beyond, taking power from the 25kV AC catenary via its pantograph. In the southbound direction this service crosses the Thames and continues down to Brighton using the 750V DC third-rail pick-up shoe. In the left foreground is the site of the former low-level platforms.

Right: A Class 66 in EWS livery makes its way along the high-level line towards Acton with a clutch of new white vans and cars. This line connects with a spur to the former GWR main line to the west near Acton.

Willesden Junction and its environs

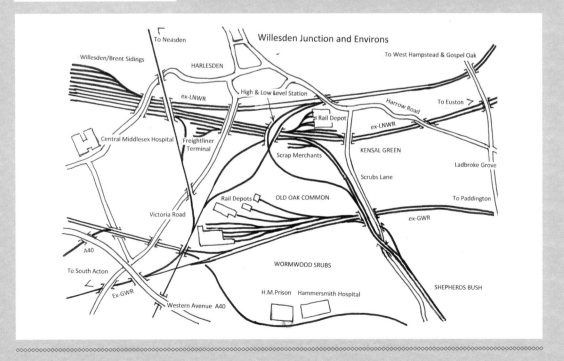

Willesden Junction and Environs

To Neasden
Willesden/Brent Sidings
HARLESDEN
To West Hampstead & Gospel Oak
ex-LNWR
High & Low Level Station
Harrow Road
To Euston
Central Middlesex Hospital
Freightliner Terminal
Rail Depot
ex-LNWR
Scrap Merchants
KENSAL GREEN
Ladbroke Grove
Scrubs Lane
Rail Depots
OLD OAK COMMON
To Paddington
Victoria Road
ex-GWR
A40
To South Acton
WORMWOOD SRUBS
SHEPHERDS BUSH
Ex-GWR
Western Avenue A40
H.M.Prison Hammersmith Hospital

The busy Traction Maintenance Depot is situated between the Transport for London DC lines and the Network Rail AC lines and opposite the former low-level platforms. Bombardier services the Class 378 EMUs as they are a part of the Bombardier Transportation Electrostar family.

Class 86 and 87 electric locomotives. Shunting in and around the yard is carried out by an ageing Class 08 diesel. The former GWR Old Oak Common engine sheds, which are just south of Willesden, are currently the TMD for the HST 125s, which were due to be replaced in 2018 by the new Crossrail nine-carriage Class 345 sets. It is proposed that the High Speed 2 line be routed past this facility.

Whatever your interest in railways may be, you cannot fail but be impressed by the constant activity from a wide diversity of lines, connections and rolling stock here.

Docklands Light Railway

The beginning

Compared with most of London's transport network, the Docklands Light Railway (DLR) is a relative newcomer. Its origins go back to the late 1960s when the once busy docks alongside the Thames in the east end of London began to decline, as imports and exports were increasingly being shipped by containers from Tilbury further down river in Essex. Eventually London Docks closed and entered a period of dereliction with dock areas used for dumping rubbish, lock gates leaking and warehouses crumbling.

In the early 1970s earnest consideration was given to redeveloping this large area for housing and business and, of course, how such a large development could be easily connected with the City through some sort of light rail system, as the Underground and National Rail network did not provide coverage.

By July 1981 the London Docklands Development Corporation (LDDC) was created by the Government to build new properties, rebuild old ones, convert warehouses into both cheaper and luxury apartments and, of course, provide a light rail network to the City.

Initial system

In 1984 decisions were made to construct the line. The track was to be standard gauge at 4ft 8½in (1,435mm), with electric traction using a third-rail, bottom-contact, 750V DC system. The rail cars were to be driverless, fully automated, with failsafe signalling under central computer control. The system would initially run 11 single-articulated rail cars manufactured by Linke-Hofmann-Busche/ BREL (now Alstom). Although the rail cars were automatic, a Passenger Service Agent (PSA) was to patrol every train to check tickets, make announcements, control the doors and take train control in the event of any failure.

In 1985 construction commenced on the initial system from a high-level, stand-alone terminus built on the site of the old Minories railway station in the City and named Tower Gateway. The line ran down the side of the river to what is now famously known as Canary Wharf, terminating at Island Gardens. A second line ran from Stratford station, an interchange with the Central Line and the National Rail network, to Island Gardens. The lines interconnected at a junction in Poplar, and short spur there ran to the DLR depot. Where possible, closed railway lines and viaducts were incorporated, together

with new structures. The line was formally opened by the Queen on 30 July 1987.

The total network was 8 miles (13km) long and comprised 15 stations.

Further extensions

Since those early days Docklands has continued to grow and passenger numbers increase annually, while Canary Wharf has become a prosperous financial centre with shopping malls, commercial businesses, bistros and restaurants. Most trains now consist of two- or three-car sets.

There have been four periods of extensions to date, with the DLR network now extending to six branches totalling 24 miles (39km) and 45

Above right: Two coupled 'B92' two-car units leave Canary Wharf station towards Heron Quays. These were first introduced between 1993 and 1995.

Right: 'B92' unit No 61 arrives at Canary Wharf heading towards Heron Quays and its final destination, Lewisham in south London.

Right: This is the view through the front window of a DLR train as it enters Canary Wharf, with West India Quay station just a short distance further on. From West India Quay the line splits left to Bank in the City and right with branches to Stratford, Beckton and Woolwich Arsenal.

Below right: Canary Wharf station is seen here with a 'B07' DLR train, first introduced in 2008, ready to leave for Bank station from the far platform, with West India Quay just a short distance beyond. The station is modern but stylish with its glass canopy ends.

stations. Another City terminus at Bank has been constructed using a tunnel to a subterranean station as an alternative to Tower Gateway, as it is more convenient for the City. Also, in 1999 an extension to Lewisham involved a new tunnel from Island Gardens under the Thames to Greenwich on the south side of the river.

The normal services offered are:

Bank to Lewisham
Bank to Woolwich Arsenal
Stratford to Canary Wharf
Stratford International to Woolwich Arsenal
Tower Gateway to Beckton (also depot and workshop)

Further extensions are proposed.

Rolling stock

Since the opening of the initial lines there have been three changes in rolling stock. The first cars used from the opening in 1987 were 11 Class 'P86s' together with 10 Class 'P89s' from 1989. The designation 'P' referred to Poplar depot. These were all withdrawn from service by 1995 and sold to EVAG in Essen, Germany, as they became unsuitable for the conditions in the expanding network.

During 1991 Bombardier built 23 cars of Class 'B90' stock, and a further 47 Class 'B92s' were introduced between 1993 and 1995. Between 2001 and 2002 another 24 cars of Class 'B2K' stock were phased in. The car designation 'B' refers to Beckton depot. These continual additions of new stock also reflected the necessary changes for wheelchair access, etc.

The last order was for 55 Class 'B07' cars from Bombardier, all of which were delivered between 2008 and 2010. Again, these cars featured a redesigned interior and exterior, larger windows and doors, better acceleration, and improved braking for a smoother ride; they can also operate in a three-car mode. Delivery of this batch was important to meet the demands of moving people to and from the Olympic Park at Stratford in 2012.

Currently there are a total of 149 cars in service on the DLR. Further orders for 43 new trains are envisaged in the near future to replace some of the early 'B90'/'B92s'. The new stock would be equivalent in length to two or three of the old stock coupled together, with walk-through carriages, air-conditioning and real-time information screens.

Top: DLR Class 'B92' No 48 is at Canary Wharf forming a train for Lewisham.

Centre: DLR Class 'B07' No 123 is also seen at Canary Wharf forming a Lewisham train. The front of the cab has a more rounded profile.

Right: Just below the DLR Canary Wharf station is the Jubilee Line tube station, which is also of modern design. It is one of the very few stations to have safety glass screening all along the edge of the platforms with designated panels that are synchronised to open only when the train doors are exactly opposite them.

Ford Motor Co, Dagenham

The Ford Motor Company plant at Dagenham was newsworthy on a regular basis during the 1960s and 1970s because of continual strikes and walk-outs caused by management and union disagreements, and of course in 1968 the women sewing machinists striking for equal pay, which they managed to achieve after vehicles continued to be manufactured without their seat covers! The BBC film *Made in Dagenham* tells this compelling story. Unfortunately, this was typical among British car manufacturing facilities at this time.

Ford 0-6-0 diesel shunter No 2, built in 1960 by RBT Stephenson Hawthorne, Works No 8098, shunts some internal-user wagons around the site.

One of the very popular and iconic Ford cars made at Dagenham between 1959 and 1967 was the Anglia 105E. It had American styling with a 997cc ohv engine, and Ford manufactured a colossal 1,004,737 vehicles. It became immortalised by model-makers Dinky Toys, Matchbox and Vanguard.

Ford originally assembled US-made car parts in an old carriage shed at Trafford Park, Manchester, but as car ownership increased a decision was made to manufacture in the UK.

It all began in May 1924 when Ford purchased the 295-acre site in Dagenham from its neighbour, Samuel Williams & Son. The site was ideal, with a 600-metre jetty with cranes that could take ships of 12,000 tons capacity. The contractor, G. Percy Trentham, had their work cut out laying roads and standard gauge railway track, and working ceaselessly to lay heavy-duty foundations for the blast furnace. Edsel Ford officially opened the site on 16 May 1929, with the first vehicle, an AA Truck, rolling off the assembly line just two years later in October 1931. From that time onwards the plant continued to grow and update its assembly

This locomotive is an 0-6-0ST built by Peckett & Sons of Bristol in 1934, Works No 1861. It was numbered as Ford's No 6 and was eventually scrapped in April 1970.

One of Ford's 0-4-0ST locomotives, a Bristol Class 4, built by Peckett & Sons, Works No 1908, is seen in 1937, delivered new to Briggs Motor Bodies, which was located on the north side of the LTSR. It was scrapped in 1965.

lines; the length of the internal railway track in 1931 was 11 miles.

During 1953 Ford acquired Briggs Motor Bodies, in Dagenham, together with its staff of 4,000, the company's site being located on the north side of the London, Tilbury & Southend Railway (LTSR) line. Briggs also had its own private railway with locomotives, but on a smaller scale than that of Ford. The number of Ford employees had now risen to approximately 40,000.

By the time the Swinging 60s came along ordinary folk were looking to buy their own cars and Ford set out to fill that need with models like the Cortina, Prefect and Anglia. By 1970 the railway had grown to 25 miles long to meet growth in manufacturing and the physical expansion of the plant. There were exchange sidings by the Dagenham Dock station on the LTSR line to cater for new vehicles being transported out of the site to the company's Liverpool Halewood Plant using the new 'Cartic' transporter wagons, and parts, etc, being transferred in. At that time Ford had a large fleet of main-line-usage wagons suitably emblazoned with the company name, as were the locomotives together with numerous internal-user wagons of many types.

However, by 2002, with the downturn in car sales and unsold cars flooding the market, the decision was made to consolidate car production

A 1940s wartime Ford poster extolling the war work that the company was carrying out to assist the war effort. A locomotive is seen with a rake of coal wagons for the internal power station and blast furnaces, beside rows of newly manufactured tractors, half-tracks and trucks for the Army.

Class 66 No 66609 leaves the exchange sidings with new vehicles heading west over the disused Chequers Road level crossing, which was made redundant by the adjacent construction work being carried out for the Channel Tunnel Rail Link, now known as High Speed 1.

and assembly in other European countries, so car assembly ceased at Dagenham, although building of diesel engines continued, with employees now numbering around 2,000. By this time the Ford railway network had diminished to 10 miles, lower than the early days of 1931.

Also, at this time construction of the High Speed 1 (HS1) railway line was taking place, which involved spurs from both up and down lines linking with the Ford sidings on the assumption that freight would be transported through the Channel Tunnel, along HS1, to the Intermodal depot at Dagenham Dock, but to date that has seldom been the case. Freight normally leaving the Channel Tunnel goes via Dollands Moor in Folkestone, where diesel locomotives take over from electric Class 92s, and uses the domestic lines through Kent.

Between its opening and 1958 the Ford plant railway operation had acquired 39 locomotives, of which 14 were 0-4-0 and 0-6-0 tank locos, 19 were diesels of various kinds, one a petrol-driven tractor, a 'Planet' diesel and a very unusual four-wheeled electric locomotive that received its power from an overhead cable and was used in the blast furnace area. Last but not least were three Bo-Bo diesel-electric locomotives built by British Thomson Houston/ Metropolitan Vickers, modelled on the American-style switchers of that time (1932). Two have been scrapped but one has been preserved on the Kent & East Sussex Railway.

Above: This is the view across the Dagenham Dock Estate to the Ford Plant from Samuel Williams & Sons' land, a business that was forced to close in 1985. Hanson Aggregates now occupies the site. Class 60 No 60029 is seen with a rake of empty PGA wagons.

Below: Ford Bo-Bo diesel-electric shunter No 1 is similar in design to an American switcher of that time and was built in 1932 by British Thomson Houston and served Ford for 34 years. It has a cab at each end with an open platform and a 'dead man's handle' for safety. Since 1966 it has resided at the Kent & East Sussex Railway.

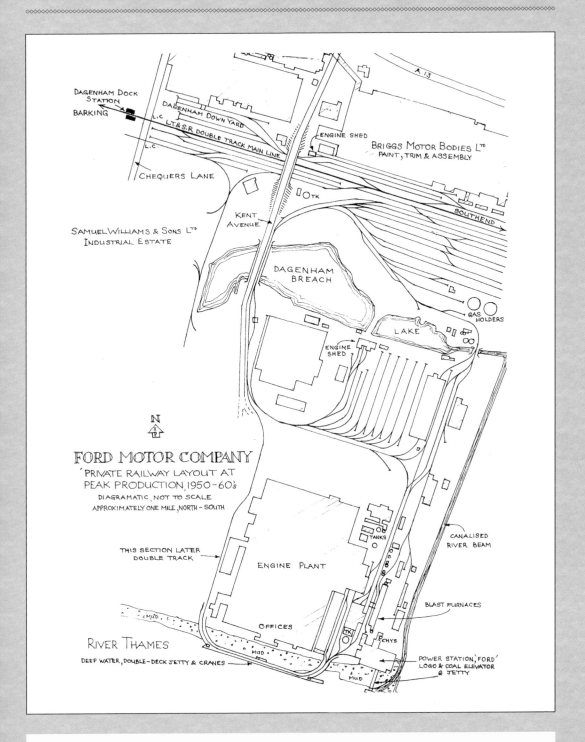

This map of the Dagenham Ford Plant shows the complexity of its internal rail network when manufacturing was at its peak during the 1950s and '60s. The London, Tilbury & Southend Railway main line runs east-west and separating Briggs Motor Bodies from Ford.

2. South and South East

The London termini serving this area outside Greater London are Victoria, Charing Cross, London Bridge, Cannon Street and St Pancras (HS1). The area currently has two main train operators, Southeastern serving Kent and East Sussex, and Southern serving some of Kent, West Sussex and Hampshire, but of course there are crossovers.

Kent has always been busy with the daily commuters and is the gateway to Europe from the port of Dover and now through the Channel Tunnel, with freight and car shuttle services from its Cheriton terminal situated just outside Folkestone.

Eurostar services from St Pancras International now use the High Speed 1 line through East London, then under the River Thames to Ebbsfleet in Kent and onwards to the Channel Tunnel and France.

East and West Sussex and some of Hampshire, apart from increasing commuters to London, have routes connecting to well-known coastal towns such as Hastings, Eastbourne, Brighton, Portsmouth and Southampton. The South Coast has always been popular for holidaymakers and day trippers, and the odd beach and pier railway adds to the attraction.

As with the rest of the country, this whole area has lost most of its picturesque branch lines, but some have been gradually brought back to life for the enjoyment of both enthusiasts and the general public.

The Channel Tunnel

Several attempts were made in the past to excavate a tunnel from England to France under the English Channel, but either technical difficulties or the threat of a foreign army coming through the tunnel and invading our green and pleasant land soon put a stop further attempts.

However, during the 1970s and early 1980s serious proposals were made and agreed by both the UK and French Governments and by 1988 the specially incorporated construction company, Trans-Marche Link (TML), had begun boring three tunnels, two large ones for standard-gauge electric trains and a smaller service tunnel in between with access to both rail tunnels. Eleven tunnel boring machines (TBMs) were used, with boring starting on both sides of the Channel. The work was duly completed and the 31.35 miles (50.45km) of tunnel was officially opened by Queen Elizabeth II and President Mitterrand of France on 6 May 1994. The French terminal was built at Coquelles, near Calais, and the English one at Cheriton, near Folkestone in Kent, and these would handle the short freight and car shuttle services, with Eurostar services having direct access to the tunnel from both ends.

Eurostar services initially ran from Paris in France and Brussels in Belgium to Waterloo station in London. Unfortunately the UK had not constructed a high-speed direct line by that time, so services through Kent and south London were routed along normal third-rail, 750V DC commuter lines as far as Factory Junction at Wandsworth Road, just south of Victoria station, where a chord was constructed to join the main lines to Waterloo. To accommodate Eurostar trains a new annex was constructed on the side of Waterloo, but became redundant once High Speed 1 (HS1) opened direct to the newly rebuilt St Pancras station. To allow the Eurostar train sets to run across Europe they were built to handle the changing power sources in different countries; 25kVA 50Hz AC, 3,000V DC, 1,500V DC and 750V DC third rail (no longer in use).

In 2010 a production of E. Nesbit's *The Railway Children* was staged in the disused

Above: At the Cheriton terminus for the Shuttle service to Coquelles, road vehicles descend access ramps to board the double-decked carrier wagons from the side. The electric Class 9 locomotives were specially constructed by Brush Traction and ABB for 25kVA operation, with a loco at each end of the train.

Above: This view shows the interior of a vehicle carrier wagon, in which cars are parked a few centimetres apart, although there is plenty of space to walk about and stretch one's legs.

Below: In 1991 the Channel Tunnel project was well under way. An observation tower was erected on the side of the M20 to give visitors an idea of the scale and progress of the Shuttle terminal. The massive concrete overbridges for vehicle access to the eight platform ramps can be seen.

Waterloo annex with tiered seats on either side of the platforms and central running track. The preserved Great Northern Railway Stirling steam locomotive No 1, a 4-2-2 built in 1870, was used, but was pushed and pulled, unseen, from the set by a Class 08 diesel outside of the stage area. Steam was generated using a fog machine.

The 68-mile (109km) High Speed 1 line (HS1) was finally opened in November 2007 and is a direct route from the tunnel, through Kent, with a stop at Ebbsfleet station. The line then descends into a tunnel under the River Thames and upon exit sweeps round east London through Stratford, terminating at St Pancras. Eurostar trains reach speeds of 186mph (109km/h) on certain stretches through the Kent countryside.

Power for HS1 and the tunnel is by 25kVA AC from an overhead catenary system via pantographs on the train sets. Eurostar sets are Classes 373 and 374, constructed by GEC Alstom and Siemens respectively.

The Shuttle Class 9 locomotives were specially designed for tunnel use and constructed by Brush Traction and ABB (ASEA Brown Boveri), and are located at each end of the train.

HS1 has also proved to be an asset for

A Eurostar Class 374, seen here at Lenham, flies down the fastest stretch of HS1 towards the Channel Tunnel. Trains can reach up to 186mph (300km/h) at this point.

commuters in Kent as specially built Hitachi Class 395 'Javelins' run a fast service to St Pancras for Southeastern. As they are dual voltage they commence their journeys from various parts of Kent using the 750V DC third rail and join the high-speed line at Ashford or Ebbsfleet (near Dartford), providing a seamless journey to London. They entered service in 2012, in time for the London Olympics.

Dollands Moor Freight Yard

Just a couple of miles west of the Channel Tunnel portal and the Shuttle terminal is Dollands Moor, a purpose-built freight yard 0.9 miles (1.4km) in length from east to west consisting of ten loop sidings capable of accommodating 0.5-mile (0.8km) trains and operated by DB Schenker. The main purpose of the yard is to provide locomotive and crew changes from electric to diesel locomotives.

At Dollands Moor in 2017 are four Class 92 electric locomotives awaiting duties. A total of 46 were built between 1993 and 1995 by Brush Traction in Loughborough; they were standard gauge and were able to operate on both 25kV AC and 750V DC using a third-rail shoe. They are also equipped to operate using both the UK and French signalling systems.

On the west side of Dollands Moor is the High Speed up line to St Pancras, and here a Eurostar Class 374 'Valero' set is quickly increasing speed having just left the Channel Tunnel from France. The tracks next to the High Speed line are of the regional 750V third-rail network to London Charing Cross and Victoria.

All lines are electrified using the same 25kVA overhead catenary system as used in the tunnel and on HS1, and also provided is 750V DC third-rail power for access to the Southeastern network to Ashford and London, etc. Dollands Moor is sandwiched between HS1 on the north side and the Southeastern Kent Coast line from Folkestone on the south side. Before HS1 was constructed to the St Pancras terminus, a link was made from the tunnel portal to the Southeastern third-rail network to enable Eurostar trains to reach Waterloo, where an annex was built to accommodate secure departures and arrivals for foreign travel. The link enabled Eurostar to switch from overhead 25kVA power to 750V DC using its third-rail shoes. The link is still in place but not in use.

Freight is currently hauled through the Channel Tunnel using permitted electric Class 92 locomotives. On entering the yard the freight wagons are temporarily held in a loop siding waiting for onward travel to London and beyond by means of an appropriate diesel locomotive, probably a Class 66.

DB Class 92 No 92015, named *D. H. Lawrence*, has hauled 20 flatbed wagons with 34 intermodal containers through the Channel Tunnel to the Eurohub terminal in Ripple Road, Barking, the last leg of the 7,456-mile (11,930km) trip from Yiwu Xi station in China to the UK. The train left China on 1 January 2017, arriving in London on the 18th.

DB Class 92 No 92011 *Handel* is still in EWS livery and also displays the outline of the old BR logo.

Isle of Grain and Glensanda

The Isle of Grain and Glensanda share two similarities, despite their being many hundreds of miles apart. Both are situated on the coast – the Isle of Grain is low-lying land on the north coast of Kent overlooking the River Thames estuary, while Glensanda is a land-locked mountainous area on Scotland's west coast. The most prestigious commonality between the two is their joint involvement in one of the world's greatest engineering projects – the rail tunnel under the English Channel to France.

Glensanda quarry, owned by Foster Yeoman,

has no road access to what is now one of the 'super league' of quarries, extracting granite, but it has a deep-water harbour, with the excavating and crushing plant concealed from the seaward side. Yeoman invested in a fleet of specialised ships, the first named *Yeoman Bridge*, which were later installed with conveyor beams to quickly discharge the cargo.

When Foster Yeoman was awarded the contract by Trans-Marche Link (TML) to supply all the aggregate for the Channel Tunnel linings in 1986 it was imperative that the company have a 'virtual' quarry in the south of England to take delivery from ships sailing from Glensanda. A site was found on the Isle of Grain in north Kent on the corner

Class 66 No 66720, named *Metronet Pathfinder*, temporarily coupled to a Foster Yeoman Class 8, is seen here awaiting its full rake of ballast wagons. Metronet Rail was a short-lived public/private company used by TFL to renew and upgrade the track, trains and signalling of nine London Underground lines until its demise in 2008.

Two GBRf Class 66s, Nos 66562 and 66505, wait at the Medway container depot adjacent to the Foster Yeoman yard.

Foster Yeoman Class 8 No 08650 *Isle of Grain* is on shunting duties at the aggregate yard. This locomotive was completed on 18 March 1959.

of the Hoo peninsula at the confluence of the estuaries of the Thames and Medway rivers. It was the derelict site of a former BP oil refinery and benefitted from a deep-water dock and connection to the national rail network. In tandem with Foster Yeoman, TML set up a large concrete works next to Foster Yeoman to manufacture the tunnel linings, with cement being supplied by Lafarge at Northfleet in Kent;

the first segments were produced in September 1987. After the curing process, the tunnel linings were loaded into bogie-box wagons and taken to the tunnel site. As the granite was unloaded from the Foster Yeoman vessels it was conveyed along the 151-metre pier to the main site where it was washed and screened before being passed to TML, or sold to other commercial users. Around two million tonnes of aggregate a year were received and processed at the Hoo site, with the last linings consignment in May 1991.

The Foster Yeoman site continued to process and distribute aggregate for the south-east of England and Railtrack, as it was at that time, then stepped up production shortly afterwards for the Channel Tunnel Rail Link (now HS1). Granite ballast was delivered for temporary storage at Beechbrook Farm, a purpose-built site just outside Ashford, with a temporary rail yard connected to the Maidstone East-Ashford third-rail line. The first HS1 section opened in 2003.

Today, Foster Yeoman, now Aggregate Industries (from 2006), continues to supply aggregate for Network Rail and others. Trains make their way up the freight-only line from the dock to Hoo Junction between Strood and Gravesend where they are marshalled in the DB Schenker yard for onward travel to Acton aggregates terminal in west London.

The Hundred of Hoo Railway

The freight-only single track running across the Isle of Grain was

Right: This photo shows two loaded trains of ballast wagons. On the left EWS Class 66 No 66186 is about to leave for an unknown Network Rail destination, while on the right the Class 08 shunter has just stopped with the next train of ballast wagons to await the arrival of its Class 66 locomotive.

Centre: The Class 08 is seen here gradually moving forward with its wagons as they are loaded with ballast by mechanical shovels and portable conveyors.

Below: Grain Crossing is at the entrance to the aggregate, oil and container terminals. This unique box was built in 1882 by Stevens & Sons and is still in daily use, but only manned when a train is due.

originally the South Eastern Railway's (SER) Hundred of Hoo branch from Gravesend to Port Victoria, which opened in 1879; a short branch to Allhallows-on-Sea was added in 1932. The railway pier at Port Victoria met the Sheerness ferry service and was a calling point for day trip paddle steamers, as well as a popular arrival and departure port for visiting Royal Families from Europe. The line closed to passenger traffic in December 1961. However, in 1923 new sidings were provided just after the Grain road crossing for the Medway Oil Storage Company's depot, proving to be a long-term lifeline for the railway. These sidings are still in use today providing the necessary rail link from Aggregate Industries, a container depot and a BP oil terminal.

Grain Crossing signal box

Being a freight-only line, the box is manned only when a train is due in or out of the container, oil or aggregate terminals that are now spread across the area. The box was built in 1882 and looks like any garden shed that requires a bit of renovation, but it is an important little structure, as it is the only surviving signal box on the entire UK railway network designed and built by Stevens & Sons. It is typified by the vertical timbering on the main walls and gable ends. The box has control over the single line, with two home signals, one fixed distant signal and the crossing gates. It is interesting to note that the signals tend to lean away from the track, as a result of subsidence.

Dover Marine station

Since the opening of the Channel Tunnel in 1994 and the increase in ferry services from Dover Eastern Docks, the former Dover Marine terminus (Western Docks) has been all but forgotten.

Dover is only 27.21 miles (43.8km) from Calais in France and has been the preferred arrival and departure port since the mid-1700s, but with the arrival of railways the race was on to open lines to Dover, which was achieved in the 1860s by two very competitive companies, the South Eastern Railway (SER) and the London, Chatham & Dover Railway (LCDR), which agreed to share the tracks on Admiralty Pier to transfer their passengers to one of their steamers. This was not ideal as the platform was open to the elements and crashing waves soaked the passengers!

In 1909 work began to construct a purpose-built undercover terminus on reclaimed land for all boat train traffic, and was completed in 1914 at the outbreak of the First World War;

Dover Marine today has been converted into a cruise ship terminal. There are no rail links to the former station, all tracks have been lifted and the area concreted over for coach access and permitted car parking. In its heyday there were six platforms, a customs hall and passenger lounges to accommodate ferry passengers disembarking to connect with a boat train to Victoria and for the arrival of boat trains from Victoria.

it did not see civilian traffic until 1920, and a full passenger service until 1922. It had four platforms to handle the increase in boat train traffic and facilities to meet and greet both foreign and British VIPs.

From 1926 it thrived with the glamour of the 'Golden Arrow' all-Pullman luxury boat train of the Southern Railway, which ran daily from London Victoria with its opulent passengers who then embarked onto the 1st Class ferry *Canterbury* to Calais. The service from Calais to Paris was by the equally luxurious French train, the 'Fleche d'Or'.

Between the wars it was decided to build a train ferry dock between Admiralty and South Quays to allow trains to be ferried across to France; this began operation in 1936 and was traditionally a night service ferrying sleeping cars and goods wagons.

The track layout at Dover was understandably complex and formed a large triangular network with main-line services arriving from London via Redhill, Ashford and Folkestone (SER) and from London via Canterbury (LCDR), together with a number of sidings for the train ferry terminal. A locomotive shed, coaling plant, turntable and marshalling yard were constructed adjacent to Dover Marine next to the line running through Shakespeare Tunnel and along the Warren to Folkestone.

In the years after the Second World War passenger numbers started to fall as the car ferry services increased from Eastern Docks, the 'Golden Arrow' service

A Southeastern Class 395 'Javelin', having just emerged from Dover Priory Tunnel, heads round the curve towards Folkestone. To the left of the photo is the disused Dover Harbour station. At this point tracks also went to the left and down to Marine station.

Dover Marine station was very busy in the days of steam. Here 'Schools' Class 4-4-0 locomotive No 3098 *St Olaves* has just left Marine station with a boat train for London Victoria via Folkestone. The line will shortly join with the line from Dover Priory station. The train is just passing under the foot passenger walkway accessible next to the Lord Warden Hotel, which closed its doors in 1939.

was withdrawn in 1972, the train ferry dock closed in 1980, and by 1994, when the Channel Tunnel opened for business, Dover Marine was closed to rail traffic for good. Marine station was refurbished and began a new lease of life as a cruise terminal.

Above: This view shows virtually the whole layout of the Dover Marine area. The old Dover Harbour station can be seen in the foreground with the lines going to the left towards Dover Priory station. The lines also curve round to the right where the photo of the Class 395 'Javelin' was taken. The train ferry terminal is in the centre of the picture with the white-painted Lord Warden Hotel to its right. Beyond is the Marine station. *Eastbank Model Railway Club*

Right: This photo shows 'Merchant Navy' Class 4-6-2 No 35019 *French Line CGT* (Compagnie Generale Transatlantique) in blue livery racing towards London with a Pullman train carrying President Auriol of France on his Presidential visit in March 1950.

Kent & East Sussex Railway

The Kent & East Sussex Railway (K&ESR) is the quintessential English branch line, which was reopened in 1974 as a preserved line. Since then it has continued to thrive, going from strength to strength, while maintaining that essential branch-line character and atmosphere as its trains puff their way through the rolling countryside and hop gardens of Kent and East Sussex.

History

Work to build the single-track, standard-gauge line was started in 1897 under the Light Railways Act of 1896, and was supervised by Colonel H. F. Stephens, who later became its General Manager, then Managing Director in 1900.

The first section of the line was opened in 1900 as the Rother Valley Railway (RVR), as it followed the course of the River Rother for part of the way. It connected Robertsbridge station on the London-Tonbridge-Hastings line of the South Eastern Railway with the Wealden market town of Tenterden, a distance of 12 miles (19km).

At Robertsbridge, then known by the RVR as Robertsbridge Junction, the line terminated at a bay platform next to the main down line. There was no run-round loop, so the train had to reverse out of the station about 300 yards (275m) to a loop on the branch line for the locomotive to run round. About half a mile (0.8km) before the station there was a short industrial spur into Hodson's Mill for delivery of coal and grain.

There were five stations between Robertsbridge and Tenterden, although from the terminus at Tenterden it was a mile (1.6km) uphill to the town. During 1903 the line was extended up a 1 in 50 incline, known as the Tenterden Bank, to Tenterden Town station, situated just 300 yards (275m) behind the High Street, and the original Tenterden station was renamed Rolvenden, and remains so today.

In 1905 a 7-mile (11.2km) extension was

This picture was taken at Tenterden station shortly after the reopening of the line in 1974, with a two-coach train hauled by ex-LB&SCR Class 'A1' 0-6-0T No 10 *Sutton*, built in 1875. These little engines were affectionately known as 'Terriers.'

opened from Tenterden Town to Headcorn, connecting with the main line between London, Tonbridge and Ashford.

The railway started operations with two new Hawthorne Leslie 2-4-0T steam locomotives and some coaches, and later bought an 0-8-0T locomotive (*Hecate*) built by Hawthorne Leslie in 1905, but at 43 tons it proved too heavy and uneconomical and eventually went to the Southern Railway in 1932, being exchanged for an 0-6-0T locomotive and two boilers. The company then changed its name from the Rother Valley Railway to the Kent & East Sussex Railway.

Unfortunately, passenger services came to an end in January 1954 and freight services in July 1961.

Hodson's Mill

The mill, which was about half a mile (0.8km) from Robertsbridge station, received its grain from Millwall Docks in bulk grain wagons that were left at the station, then a K&ESR locomotive would shunt them down the branch to the spur and into the mill. A day after British Rail closed the line to freight a delivery of grain was left at Robertsbridge station with no locomotive to take the wagons to the mill. BR said it would have to unload the wagons at the station, which of course was impossible. The company, tongue in cheek, said to BR, 'You find us a locomotive and we will run it to the mill ourselves.' Lo and behold, a 'P' Class 0-6-0 tank locomotive, No 31556, built in 1909 for the South Eastern & Chatham Railway, was found in Brighton and duly delivered to Robertsbridge, but there was nobody at the mill who could drive a steam locomotive. Reminiscent of *The Titfield Thunderbolt*, the local policeman was walking by and, upon

enquiring what was going on, said that he used to be a fireman on 0-6-0 'Terriers' at Newhaven Docks and would be pleased to assist them and provide instructions to the mill workers. They named the locomotive *The Pride of Sussex* and the operation then ran without mishaps until BR dismantled the track in 1970. The locomotive is now on the preserved K&ESR.

The Kent & East Sussex Railway in preservation

In 1971 the Tenterden Railway Company (now The Kent & East Sussex Railway) was incorporated and bought the land, at a cost of £60,000, to begin the task of reopening the line between Tenterden and Bodiam. The 10½-mile (16.8km) line was reopened in stages, in view of the fact that the track, bridges, crossings and stations all required rebuilding or extensive repair. The first section was opened to Rolvenden on 1 June 1974 with the final section to Bodiam on 2 April 2000. From Tenterden Town the stations are Rolvenden, Wittersham Road, Northiam and Bodiam, with the wonderful vista from the station across the sleepy Rother valley to the 600-year-old Bodiam Castle.

The line is now closed just past Bodiam and

Hodson's Mill at Robertsbridge had its own 'P' Class 0-6-0T locomotive originally built in 1909 for the South Eastern & Chatham Railway. It is seen here pushing a bulk grain wagon into the mill for unloading.

the section between the old A21 by Hodson's Mill up to Robertsbridge station is now owned by the Rother Valley Railway, which is building a new station and already has a track connection to the national network. It is now a distinct probability that this remaining 3½ miles (5.6km) of derelict line will once more, in spite of some major obstacles, be reopened to see trains run from Tenterden to Robertsbridge.

Rolling stock

The K&ESR has a number of serviceable steam locomotives that are in keeping with a light railway, with just a couple of exceptions.

There are also diesel locomotives including shunters and a GWR railcar dating back to 1940. The railway also has a number of vintage coaches dating back from the late 1800s to the early 1900s, all beautifully renovated.

The French connection

The K&ESR is twinned with its nearest preserved railway neighbour in Normandy, France, the Chemin de Fer de la Baie de Somme, and on occasions locomotives are exchanged for gala weekends, etc.

Top: This intriguing little Sentinel locomotive (Works No 6807), No 10 *Gervase*, was built in 1928. It has a vertical boiler and chain drive. For its size its pulling power is impressive.

Centre: This ex-Norwegian State Railways 2-6-0 tender loco was built in Sweden in 1919 and given the number 376. After extensive reworking it was renamed *Norwegian*.

Right: Hodson's Mill's 'P' Class 0-6-0T locomotive has taken on water from a rather inadequate hosepipe. It now carries the name *Pride of Sussex*, which was the brand name of the flour produced at the mill.

In the early days of the K&ESR Colonel Stephens introduced an 0-8-0T locomotive, *Hecate*, built by Hawthorne Leslie in 1905, but at 43 tons it prove too heavy and uneconomical to run and was taken over by the Southern Railway in 1932.

Above: An ex-BR Class 108 DMU is just leaving Tenterden station for Bodiam during July 2010. The K&ESR took over the DMU in 1993.

Right: 'USA' Class No 65, built in America in 1943, was shipped across to the UK in kit form as part of the war effort. After the war it spent time on shunting duties around Southampton Docks and eventually arrived on the K&ESR as a preservation project in 1968.

Right: This endearing little locomotive is an 0-4-0 side tank built in 1923 by Peckett of Bristol and is named *Marcia*. It is seen here taking on water in Rolvenden yard.

Centre: 'David and Goliath' at Bodiam during the May 2011 Gala. Visiting locomotive GWR 4-4-0 *City of Truro* looms over the K&ESR's 'A1X' 'Terrier' No 32678, built in Brighton to a Stroudley design in 1880.

Bottom left: Flying down the bank from Northiam into Wittersham Road station in 2012 is GWR Class '16xx' 0-6-0 pannier tank No 1638 designed by Hawksworth and built in Swindon Works in 1951.

Bottom right: Two locomotives back to back are just about to leave with 'The Wealden Pullman' in 2010. The lead loco is 'P' Class side tank 0-6-0 No 753 built at Ashford Works in 1909. The second loco is 'P' Class 0-6-0 No 32678.

Opposite top: The K&ESR has among its collection a GWR railcar. An example is seen here at Moreton-in-Marsh, Gloucestershire, with a steam-hauled train approaching.

Opposite bottom: At Hodson's Mill near Robertsbridge on the K&ESR, a 'P' Class and a 'Terrier' shunt wagons of coal, a scene sadly never to be repeated.

Romney, Hythe & Dymchurch Railway

Living as I do in the County of Kent, an occasional visit to the Romney, Hythe & Dymchurch Railway (RHDR) is always a delightful experience.

The RHDR is a 15-inch-gauge (381mm) light railway that was opened in 1927 and provides a year-round public service as well as catering for the tourist trade. The line is 13½ miles (21.7km) long and runs south-west along the Kent coast between the Cinque Port of Hythe and Dungeness via stations at Dymchurch, St Mary's Bay, Romney Warren, New Romney and Romney Sands. The journey time is about 1 hour 5 minutes each way and the trains are normally steam-hauled except certain times in the winter and for the early morning contracted school runs from Hythe to New Romney and back. The locomotives can safely haul trains up to 25mph (40kph) on the narrow-gauge track.

The line was the brainchild of two railway visionaries, Captain Jack Howey and Count Zborowski; the latter was a racing driver,

This Canadian Pacific-style locomotive is No 9 *Winston Churchill*, resplendent in its red livery. It is approaching Hythe terminus in 2014 with a train from Dungeness and is looking very 'main line', with the signal box on the left.

but died in a motor racing accident in Monza before any location for a railway was decided, leaving Jack with two ready-built locomotives and nowhere to run them. The locomotives were designed by Henry Greenly and built by Davey, Paxman & Co of Colchester, Essex. The Romney Marsh site was eventually chosen and an 8-mile (12.8km) double-track line was opened between Hythe and New Romney on 16 July 1927.

The opening was a grand affair attended by the mayors of both towns, and the first train was hauled by *Hercules*, a 4-8-2 built in 1927. The double track was then extended another 5½ miles (8.8km) from New Romney to Dungeness.

Winston Churchill is turned on the turntable at Hythe in readiness for a return journey to Dungeness. This beautiful 4-6-2 was built by Davey, Paxman of Colchester and the Yorkshire Engine Company of Sheffield and came into service in 1931 as *Doctor Syn*; the name was changed in 1948.

At the start of the Second World War the line was taken over by the military and a miniature armoured train was built that housed an anti-tank rifle and Lewis guns. The War Department at the time considered the train to be of critical advantage, as it could relocate quickly along the coast line to where it was needed. It also protected the coast line during the laying of the under-sea fuel line from Dungeness to Ambleteuse on the Pas-de-Calais, France, after D Day. This was part of the PLUTO operation (Pipe Line Under The Ocean). It all sounds very 'Dad's Army' today, but perhaps the little train put a few shells through the wings of enemy planes!

Seen in 2016, this is No 10 *Doctor Syn*, a 4-6-2 in the same Canadian Pacific styling as No 9 and built in Sheffield by the Yorkshire Engine Company in 1931. Dr Syn was an infamous fictitious Dymchurch smuggling vicar.

After the war the line was returned by the War Department to the RHDR, but was now a single track from New Romney to Dungeness due to war damage. The line reopened again in 1946 from Hythe to New Romney, and from New Romney to Dungeness, as a single track; in 1947 it was Laurel and Hardy who cut the ribbon.

The railway has 11 steam locomotives, eight 4-6-2s, two 4-8-2s and one 0-4-0. Seven were built by Davey, Paxman & Co between 1925 and 1927, two by the Yorkshire Engine Company in 1931, one by Krauss of Munich in 1926, and one by Krupp of Essen in 1937.

Above left: No 14 *Captain Howey* is a main-line diesel loco named after one of the founders of the RH&DR. It is a 112bhp, six-cylinder Bo-Bo diesel engine, and is seen here in 2012 at Dungeness station.

Left: No 5 *Hercules* takes a breather at New Romney station in 2008. The locomotive was built as a 4-8-2 in 1927 by Davey, Paxman of Colchester.

Hercules and No 2 *Northern Chief* are steamed up and ready to go at New Romney station in 2008.

There are also two diesel-mechanical locos of Bo-Bo wheel arrangements built by TMA Engineering in 1983 and 1989.

The railway carries more than 100,000 passengers a year in its well-maintained assortment of open and closed carriages.

At the far end of the line is Dungeness station, which has been tastefully rebuilt with a new shop and cafeteria. The line is still single track from New Romney to Dungeness, but the need to turn a locomotive or have a run-round loop is avoided as the station is located on a circular loop that rejoins the single main line, after a few hundred yards, for the return journey. Dungeness is certainly different and has a compelling and perhaps eerie attraction, which draws visitors back again and again.

Today, the Romney, Hythe & Dymchurch Railway is a fine example of working history and has managed to survive, regenerate and improve over the last 90 years. It has much to offer as a tourist attraction in Kent and is definitely a main line in miniature!

4-6-2 No 2 *Northern Chief* was built in 1926 by Davey, Paxman and is seen here taking on water for its next journey.

Volk's Electric Railway, Brighton

We all like a day at the seaside, but there are not many resorts where a railway runs along the beach for the pleasure of tourists. The Volk's Electric Railway (VER) in Brighton on the south coast is one in particular that deserves a mention. It is now operated by Brighton & Hove City Council with assistance from Volk's Electric Railway Association (VERA), who carry out practical tasks including maintenance and promotional work.

The VER is the oldest operating electric railway in the world and was constructed by the inventor Magnus Volk in 1883. Since then it has undergone three track gauge changes and as many electric power changes, resulting in a gauge of 2ft 8½in (825mm), and is electrified at 110V DC from a third rail situated between the tracks and favouring one side.

The track is only 1¼ miles (2km) in length and runs from Aquarium station, next to the Palace Pier, to Black Rock station, just short of Brighton Marina, with an intermediate halt at

Above: Full with delighted passengers, car No 7, coupled to lead car No 8, is nearing its terminus just short of Brighton's Palace Pier. The trains travel most of the way immediately next to the promenade.

Right: Empty coupled cars Nos 7 and 8 are seen at the Palace Pier terminus waiting for their next passengers for the 1¼-mile (2km) trip to Black Rock station.

Cars Nos 7 and 8 are on their way to Palace Pier terminus full of passengers. Note the driving wheel and the 110V DC third rail that is positioned just inside the running rail.

Halfway, which is also the car shed and depot. However, all is about to change because in 2016 work began to rebuild Aquarium station to incorporate a heritage visitor centre, and to provide a new car shed at Halfway to include a conservation workshop for restoration training. All this has been funded by the Heritage Lottery Fund. The railway was expected to be fully operational for the 2018 season.

At the time of writing the rolling stock consists of three 40-seat semi-open motorised cars built by the VER between 1901 and 1926, numbering 7, 8 and 9 and using Compagnie Electrique Belge 8hp motors. Motorised cars Nos 4, 6 and 10 are nearing the completion of their restoration.

Because of the very low train speed, signalling is not required as there are two passing loops for trains that have started from each end of the line, and there is only one train on the single-line sections. Communication is by radio between drivers and the control.

Shawford railway accident

On 20 July 1952 on a stretch of line just west of Shawford station between Eastleigh and Winchester in Hampshire, where four tracks reduce to two, the driver of a local train overran a home signal causing the locomotive to be derailed by a protective catch point and a sand drag. The train, hauled by 'Lord Nelson' Class 4-6-0 *Howard of Effingham* (built at Eastleigh in 1926-29), was travelling at 30mph on the up slow line and should have been held at signals to allow a boat train to pass on the up fast line. However, it appears that the driver misread and then overran the gantry home signal, but a major crash was averted as the catch point protected the fast line and derailed the locomotive and the first coach, which fell some 20 feet (7 metres) onto their sides down an embankment. There were 70 passengers on board, but there were no injuries, and both the driver and fireman managed to jump clear. The train guard ran back down the track and set detonators on the

Right: This was the sorry sight of the 1928-built 'Lord Nelson' Class 4-6-0 No 854 *Howard of Effingham* lying on its side, waiting for some temporary track to be laid to enable it to be hauled up the embankment to the running track. Plenty of locals including kids are taking a keen interest in these very unusual proceedings.

rails as a warning to any following trains that an accident had occurred.

The next task was to safely recover the slightly damaged locomotive, so a ramp was built with a short piece of track, and once the locomotive was righted by using timber baulks it was winched back up to the slow line. The 'Lord Nelson' Class had all been withdrawn from service by 1962.

As the accident happened in the school holidays, word soon got about and many people came to visit this unusual occurrence; there was only one policeman on duty, so many youngsters had a great time exploring and watching the recovery. Health and safety was unheard of in those days!

Above right: Howard of Effingham has now been manoeuvred into the upright position with the aid of jacks and heavy timber sleepers, making it ready for the next tricky stage of recovery. The locals are certainly very close to the action but nobody seems to mind. On the embankment is a brake van of the Engineer's Breakdown Train from the nearby Eastleigh Works.

Right: The temporary ramp and track complete, *Howard Effingham* is now ready to be winched up to the running line at the top of the embankment. Today this would have been labelled a 'dangerous operation' and all spectators removed, but nobody had heard of health and safety in 1952!

Finally, *Howard of Effingham* has regained some dignity at the top of the incline, albeit with a few dents and a bent smoke deflector. A Bulleid 'Pacific' of the 'West Country' Class heads its train from Southampton on the up line to London via Winchester while a lone 1952-style constable in appropriate helmet looks on.

Hythe Ferry Pier Railway, Southampton

As ocean liners like *Queen Elizabeth 2* come into their berths at the international port of Southampton, they dwarf the red and white Hythe Ferry boats that dart across Southampton Water from Hythe to the town quay at Southampton. There has been a ferry service between these two points since the 16th century.

Hythe is a small, pleasant town on the west bank of the Solent, fringed by the New Forest Park. Some of its famous inhabitants included Lawrence of Arabia and Sir Christopher Cockrell, inventor of the hovercraft.

An iron pier was constructed in 1879 and opened for business on 1 January 1881. The pier happens to be the seventh longest in the UK and the pier railway holds the record as being the world's oldest still in use. The single-track railway of 2-foot (610mm) gauge runs the

Built in 1909, the 640-metre-long pier had its railway installed in 1922 and is the world's longest continuously running pier railway.

A train returns from the pier head having met the regular ferry from Southampton across Southampton Water.

full length of the pier, some 700 yards (640m). A third rail delivers 250V DC to two small locomotives built by the Brush Electrical Co of Loughborough in 1909 for the opening of the line.

There are three coaches, one of which is also equipped with a cramped driving cab, as the loco is positioned at the landward end. There is also a short platform wagon for carrying large luggage and for track maintenance purposes. At the station there is a single siding that leads into the workshops, which has no third rail, necessitating manual shunting.

A half-hourly service is run on a 25-minute round trip connecting with the ferry boat.

A view of the pier from an Isle of Wight ferry.

Island Line train No 6, of 1938 tube stock, halts at Brading station en route to Ryde Pier Head. The nearer island platform is now unused and the track has been removed; it once served as the terminal platform for the St Helens/Bembridge branch line, which closed in 1953. Brading station has a small railway museum and the signal box that is still complete and can be visited at certain times.

Isle of Wight railways

Island Line

Situated just 2 miles off the Hampshire coast, separated by a stretch of sea known as the Solent in the English Channel, the Isle of Wight has been a popular holiday destination since Victorian times. Connection to the mainland is by various ferry services from Cowes, Ryde and Yarmouth, and from 1862 five railway companies gradually built a rail network around the island to transport goods and passengers to the other towns and holiday resorts including Sandown, Shanklin and Ventnor. By 1901 a total of 55½ miles (89km) of mainly single-line track had been laid. In 1880 the Ryde-Ventnor line was extended to the end of Ryde Pier for the onward travel of passengers from the ferries. All services were steam-hauled and the locomotives required a large amount of coal, which was shipped from the mainland to Cowes then up the Medina River to Medina Wharf, Newport. From there it was distributed to convenient points on the network together with necessary domestic supplies. During the steam era only tank engines were used and consisted of several Class 'A1' 0-6-0Ts (ex-LBSCR) and 23 Class 'O2' 0-4-4Ts (ex-LSWR). Each locomotive was named after a town on the Island and uniquely numbered with a preceding 'W' (for example, No W33 *Bembridge*).

But of course the Island was subject to the changes that took place in the railways on the mainland and following the 1923 Grouping all services were operated by the Southern Railway; after nationalisation in 1948 it became part of British Railways Southern Region. Following various modernisation schemes and the Beeching Report, all but the Ryde-Shanklin line had been closed by 1966. This remaining line

Island Line train No 6, bound for Shanklin, has just left Ryde Esplanade and is running down into Ryde Tunnel, 396 yards (362m) in length and built in 1881 under the Esplanade. It originally had two portals but with the advent of just two trains on the single track only one portal is in use.

was then to be electrified using 43 'old' Class 485 and 486 tube train stock from 1927 to 1934 built by Metropolitan-Cammell, which had previously worked on the London Underground. It appears that this stock was chosen because its lower height allowed it to travel through the reduced headroom of the Ryde Tunnel, as no electric BR stock was suitable.

The line was temporarily closed between 1 January and 19 March 1967 to allow for the installation of the 630V DC third-rail electrification, and the trains had to be modified from the original four-rail traction current where the centre rail was used for the return. Also, track heights were raised at stations to accommodate the low floors of the tube trains. In 1985 the line was branded as RydeRail.

During 1990 onwards all of the older trains were replaced by a newer fleet (already 50 years old) of eight two-car sets of Class 483 London tube stock built by Metro-Cammell in 1938 and numbered 483001-008. They were extensively refurbished at Eastleigh Works and converted to third-rail operation. The line was rebranded as the Island Line, replacing the former RydeRail brand. In 1992 a ninth set was delivered, together with a tenth for spare parts.

In 1996 privatisation of the UK's railways also included the Isle of Wight, which became the Island Line franchise, and in 2007 became a part of the South Western franchise, and services have continued to run under the name

Island Line train No 6 has just left Ryde Pier Head station heading towards Ryde Esplanade. Turn-around time at Ryde Pier is 5 minutes. Trains become busy when foot passengers disembark from the ferry from the mainland. The total journey time to Shanklin is about 25 minutes to travel the 8½ miles (13.6km).

Island Line Trains. This old stock is now being replaced by Vivarail Class 484 units, rebuilt from LU 1980 stock.

The line is 8½ miles (13.6km) from Ryde Pier Head to Shanklin, and the journey takes about 23 minutes, with intermediate stations at Ryde Esplanade, Ryde St John's Road (depot), Smallbrook Junction, Brading, Sandown and Lake. Trains stop at Smallbrook Junction at specified times only to allow passengers to transfer to and from the heritage Isle of Wight Steam Railway, as there is no public access to the station other than by rail. Maintaining the current timetable requires two trains in service on the single track, with passing places at Ryde St John's Road and Sandown stations, and a turn-round time of about 6 minutes at each end of the line providing two trains every hour in each direction.

Isle of Wight Steam Railway

The Isle of Wight Steam Railway is a heritage railway that runs along the original single-track Ryde & Newport Railway, which was opened on 20 December 1875 and was amalgamated with the Cowes & Newport Railway in 1887 to form the Isle of Wight Central Railway. Although a valuable asset to the local population, the railway handled a relatively low level of traffic, as did most of the Island's network, and under recommendations from the Beeching Report the line was closed in 1966.

However, all was not lost as the Wight Locomotive Society raised funds to buy one of the last remaining steam locomotives, No W24 *Calbourne*, and some carriages. In 1971 the Isle

of Wight Railway Co Ltd was formed with the objective of buying 1½ miles (2.4km) of track between Wootton and Havenstreet. Today the very rural 5½-mile (8.8km) line extends from Wootton through to Havenstreet (Head Office and Depot), terminating at Smallbrook Junction, where a run-round loop is provided for a locomotive. The Isle of Wight Steam Railway has its own dedicated platform with a short walkway across to the Island Line platform that lies parallel to it.

The rolling stock consists of some of the early ex-London, Brighton & South Coast Railway's 0-6-0T Class 'A1s' (Nos W8 *Freshwater* and W11 *Newport*) and the London & South Western Railway's 0-4-4T Class 'O2' No W24 *Calbourne*, which had been shipped across to the Island in the early part of the 1900s. A varied selection of Hunslet Austerity 0-6-0Ts and LMS Ivatt Class 2 2-6-2T locomotives and diesels, together with numerous coaches and wagons, make up the remainder of the rolling stock.

Ex-British Rail Class 03 0-6-0DM diesel locomotive No D2059, built in 1959 and carrying the late BR crest, pulls into Havenstreet station with the last train of the day. The original Southern Railway carriages are looking pristine in the late afternoon sun.

Left: Having uncoupled from its train at Havenstreet, the 03 is being shunted onto its overnight siding while being admired by several onlookers.

Below: Beautifully turned-out LMS Ivatt Class 2 2-6-2T No 41313, built in 1952, returns from Smallbrook after a test run. She was withdrawn from service in 1965 at Eastleigh and went for scrap at Woodham Brothers at Barry, but was then rescued and restored to this immaculate condition by 2017.

Ex-LSWR Class 'O2' 0-4-4T No W29 *Alverstone*, built at Nine Elms in 1891, was transferred to the Island in 1926. It is seen here at Ryde shed in the late 1950s. *Peter Lambert*

Ex-LSWR Class 'O2' 0-4-4T No W14 *Fishbourne*, built at Nine Elms in 1889, was transferred to the Island in 1936 and is seen here running round at a sunny Ventnor in the 1950s. *Peter Lambert*

This 1960s photo shows two of the early Class 485 1927 tube stock units built by Metropolitan-Cammell and converted to third-rail 630V operation at Ryde Pier Head station. The service was then called RydeRail.

Above: An unidentified Class 'O2' leaves Ryde Esplanade and heads down the 1 in 50 gradient towards Ryde Tunnel with a train bound for Ventnor. *Peter Lambert*

Below left: Ex-LSWR Class 'O2' 0-4-4 No W18 *Ningwood*, built at Nine Elms in 1892, was transferred to the Island in 1930 and is seen here resting at Ryde shed. *Peter Lambert*

Below right: Sister loco No W21 *Sandown*, built at Nine Elms in 1891 and transferred to the Island in 1924, is seen at an unknown location. *Peter Lambert*

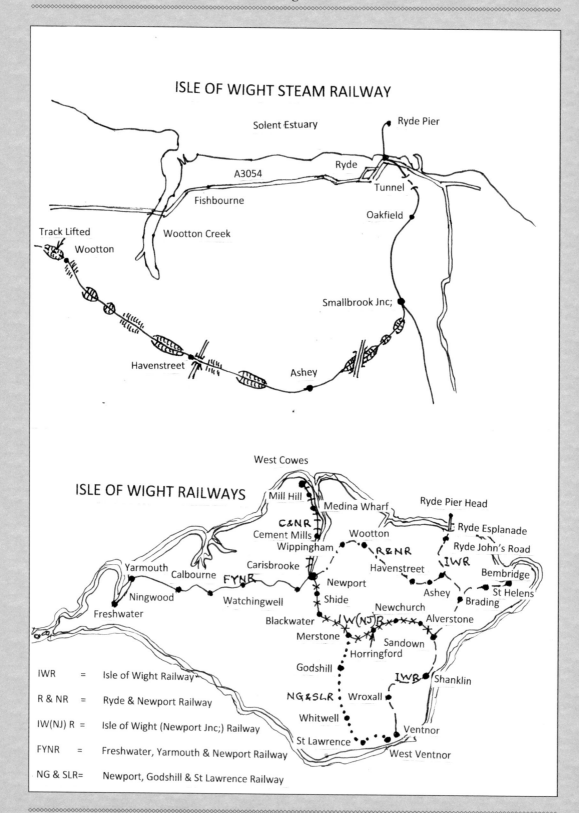

ISLE OF WIGHT STEAM RAILWAY

ISLE OF WIGHT RAILWAYS

IWR	=	Isle of Wight Railway
R & NR	=	Ryde & Newport Railway
IW(NJ) R	=	Isle of Wight (Newport Jnc;) Railway
FYNR	=	Freshwater, Yarmouth & Newport Railway
NG & SLR=		Newport, Godshill & St Lawrence Railway

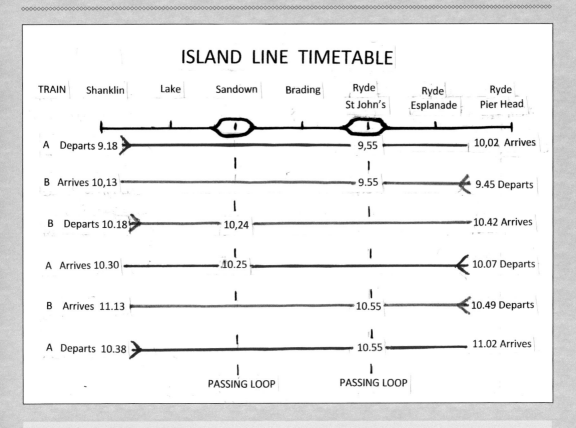

ISLAND LINE TIMETABLE

TRAIN	Shanklin	Lake	Sandown	Brading	Ryde St John's	Ryde Esplanade	Ryde Pier Head
A	Departs 9.18				9,55		10,02 Arrives
B	Arrives 10,13				9.55		9.45 Departs
B	Departs 10.18		10,24				10.42 Arrives
A	Arrives 10.30		10.25				10.07 Departs
B	Arrives 11.13				10.55		10.49 Departs
A	Departs 10.38				10.55		11.02 Arrives

PASSING LOOP   PASSING LOOP

Nuclear flask trains

The UK still relies on nuclear power stations to supply the national grid system with electrical power. They are situated at Heysham, Wylfa, Hinkley Point, Oldbury, Hunterston, Torness, Hartlepool, Dungeness and Sizewell.

The reactors use radioactive fuel rods, which require to be changed on a regular basis, as their working life diminishes. The used rods are extremely radioactive and contain uranium and plutonium and are stored in cooling ponds at the power station until they can be transported to Sellafield in Cumbria for reprocessing.

When ready, the rods are placed in large water-filled lead-lined steel containers called flasks. The lid is then secured to prevent them being accessed during transit. Each flask weighs 50 tons and before leaving the nuclear site they are washed down with water to remove any radioactive contamination that may be on the surface. The flasks are then taken to the nearest railhead by lorry for loading onto specially prepared flatbed railway wagons that carry just one flask each.

A flask was tested for safety in the 1980s in a staged head-on rail crash at 64mph (102km/h) and came out unscathed, apart from a little superficial damage, whereas the diesel locomotive that hit it and the flatbed wagon were virtually destroyed.

The railhead at Dungeness in Kent is a secure area just large enough for two diesel locomotives and two wagons. It is security fenced all round with a gantry crane system to lift and manipulate the flasks off the lorry and onto the wagons. The railhead is situated at the end of the 1¼-mile (2 km) access road to the power station, and is separated by the Lydd Town/Dungeness road. The whole operation is open to public view, but the actual timetable is not publicised.

The flask train is the responsibility of Direct Rail Services (DRS), which is publicly owned by the Nuclear Decommissioning Authority (NDA). DRS uses Class 20, Class 37 or sometimes Class 66 and Class 68 diesels for this

The nuclear flasks are seen here at Dungeness having just been loaded on to their specially built individual flat wagons. They are transported a short distance from the power station by road and the gantry crane positions them on the flat wagons. The site is securely fenced.

purpose, and they are always used in pairs as a precaution against failure en route. The service was previously provided under the ownership of British Nuclear Fuels Ltd (BNFL), but transferred to the NDA on its creation on 1 April 2004.

The Dungeness train used two Class 37s, Nos 37218 and 37612. Once the locomotives were coupled to the two flatbed wagons the whole train was reversed back so that the front gates could be secured until the train was due to depart about 50 minutes later.

The single line from Dungeness to Appledore is part of the original Appledore to Lydd railway and is now used only for the flask trains that run once or twice a week. It is a route of approximately 10 miles (16km) across Romney Marshes, a flat but attractive landscape with medieval churches, green fields, water-filled dykes and thousands of Romney Marsh sheep. There are 11 open crossings (no barriers or lights) along the way to provide access for the narrow country lanes with grass growing down the middle, mainly used by local farmers and the few private dwellings in the area.

When the train arrives at the junction with the Marshlink line (Ashford-Brighton) at Appledore, it waits on the branch for clearance to proceed into the small unmanned station platform. When clearance is received the crossing barriers are automatically lowered over the B2080 road adjacent to the station and the train accelerates quickly away towards Ashford with its dangerous but secure cargo.

Leaving Ashford the train then makes its way through Kent to London, then to Willesden in the north-west of the capital, which is also the marshalling point for the Sizewell waste. The train then travels north to Sellafield. En route there may well be a 'layover' site where the train waits to be slotted into an allotted schedule.

As far as the other nuclear power stations are concerned, both Hartlepool, Hunterston and Torness are marshalled at Carlisle, with Hinkley Point and Wylfa marshalled at Warrington. Heysham is direct. As Sellafield is on the west coast, all of the nuclear flask rail routes feed into the West Coast Main Line.

After delivery to Sellafield, a train is then scheduled to return the empty flasks to Dungeness in readiness for the next journey north.

Above: The two Direct Rail Services (DRS) Class 37s, Nos 37612 and 37218, sit idling waiting for the security gates to be opened so that they can couple to the two nuclear flask wagons.

Right: Once coupled to the flask wagons the two Class 37s wait for clearance to proceed along the single track towards Appledore station on the Marshlink line.

Below right: This view along the old Appledore and Lydd railway line is looking towards Appledore – a reasonably straight stretch of single track with 11 open crossings!

British Rail Class 37

A total of 309 locomotives were built for British Rail between 1960 and 1965 by English Electric at its Vulcan Foundry at Newton-le-Willows and Robert Stephenson & Hawthorn of Darlington.

They have been used for both passenger and freight work with a top speed of 90mph (144km/h). They have a Co-Co configuration, and the transmission is diesel-electric with English Electric DC traction motors. The power output is 1,750bhp (1,305kW). Over the years the locomotives have had major overhauls and refurbishments with generators being

replaced by alternators, rewiring and new engines. These various changes have given rise to six sub-classes of the original Class 37. Apart from those still in commercial service, approximately 50 have survived the breaker's yard and are privately owned, or with heritage railway groups across the UK.

Locomotive No 37218 was built at the Vulcan Foundry and went into service with BR in January 1965. It was used extensively in many parts of England and headed railtours and latterly worked Railfreight trains. It was then allocated to EWS (English Welsh & Scottish) in September 1998 and finally

allocated to DRS in October 2003.

Locomotive No 37612, a later locomotive, went into service with BR in October 1963 and spent most of its working life in and around Wales and heading the occasional railtour. No working information is available after February 1987.

Right: One of the crossings demonstrates the multitude of different signs to supposedly assist the local motorist or pedestrian to beware of a train that only runs once or twice a week!

Below: Here the two Class 37s are coming off the Appledore-Lydd line, crossing the Marshlink line into Appledore station, which is unmanned.

Once in Appledore station the train waits to receive instructions to proceed to Ashford for onward travel to London and its eventual destination of Sellafield.

3. South West, West and Wales

This large area is served by two major termini from London, namely Waterloo and Paddington. Currently South Western Railway from Waterloo utilises some of the old London & South Western Railway routes through Berkshire, Hampshire and down to the Jurassic coast at Weymouth in Dorset and Exeter in Devon. These routes are largely 750V DC third rail using electric multiple units (EMUs) as far as Weymouth, thereafter diesel multiple units (DMUs) are used.

Paddington station is the preserve of the Great Western Railway (GWR), although the Heathrow Express also operates from there. GWR main routes today are not very different from the early days, reaching places like Reading, Swindon, Bath, Bristol, Taunton, Exeter and through to Plymouth and Penzance at the tip of Cornwall. The main line continues from Bristol through the Severn Tunnel and into South Wales to Cardiff, Swansea and Carmarthen. Other routes go to Worcester, Hereford, Cheltenham and Oxford. The GWR network is almost reliant on diesel traction using InterCity 125 sets that were first introduced in 1975 and are still going strong, although some of the Paddington main line to Bristol is now partly electrified using the 25kV overhead catenary system. It now seems that a decision has been made to put a temporary hold on electrifying the line any further and to use bi-mode sets instead.

Although GWR runs the main-line services to Swansea, all other local services in North and South Wales are served by Arriva Trains Wales and interchange with other train operating companies at places such as Birmingham, Manchester and Crewe.

This section covers the interesting business of the Cornish clay industry and the reinvention of a Devon branch line. Although Wales no longer has its many coal mines and branch lines transporting coal down the valleys to Barry and Cardiff docks, it has magnificent scenery, especially to the north, with some wonderful preserved narrow-gauge railways that once carried slate and stone and are now enjoyed by enthusiasts and tourists alike.

The 'Devon Belle'

There have been many named trains over the years, but only one 'Devon Belle'. It was introduced by the Southern Railway on Friday 20 June 1947 at 12 noon when it left Waterloo for Ilfracombe in north Devon with its rake of Pullman carriages and rear observation car.

The 12 noon 'Devon Belle' is ready to leave Waterloo in 1948. The locomotive is Bulleid Merchant Navy class 4-6-2 No 35003 *Royal Mail SR No 21C3*.

The Waterloo-bound 'Devon Belle' makes its way down Honiton bank towards Seaton Junction behind an unidentified 'Merchant Navy' Class loco. One of the two unique and exclusive observation cars is attached to the rear of the train of 13 Pullman coaches. *Mike Morant collection*

The normal route was the old LSWR line via Basingstoke, Yeovil, Honiton and Exeter. On its arrival at Exeter Central at 3.35pm, the train was split, the front portion going on to Plymouth and the rear portion and observation car continuing to Ilfracombe, arriving at 5.27pm. The same was done in reverse for the up train, which left Ilfracombe at 12 noon, arriving at Waterloo at 5.20pm. Trains ran every Friday, Saturday, Sunday and Monday.

At the outset trains consisted of ten Pullman carriages, including the observation car, splitting at Exeter with four for Plymouth and six, including the observation car, for Ilfracombe. As the train proved very popular, especially during holiday periods, it was increased to 12 carriages, four for Plymouth and eight, including the observation car, for Ilfracombe. This consist allowed for 70 1st Class and 138 2nd Class passengers, with every seat having a dining table. Every pair of carriages had its own kitchen and pantry for serving quality meals. As expected, the interior of the carriages was in typical Pullman style with marquetry wall panels, table lamps and comfortable seating. There was 22 Pullman staff on each train, including an attendant for each carriage and the conductor.

The observation cars were rebuilt from two different vehicles. One started life as a 1918 LNWR ambulance car and the other an ordinary 3rd Class carriage, both being rebuilt by the Pullman Company with comfortable seating for 27 passengers, refreshment buffet and kitchen. They were single-ended with a large picture window across the rear end for panoramic visibility, which meant that they had to be turned on a turntable for the return journey.

The carriages were named in the usual Pullman way, including *Rosamond*, *Argus*, *Geraldine*, *Iolanthe* and *Minerva*, and were cleaned every morning at 6.00am by nine men.

The 'Devon Belle' was always hauled by SR 'Merchant Navy' Class locomotives, mainly with the original air-smoothed casing that led to their nickname 'Spam cans'!

By the early 1950s passenger numbers started to decline, probably as would-be passengers were now buying small family cars to holiday in Devon. Operating days were reduced and sadly the 'Devon Belle' was finally withdrawn in September 1954 after a short life, but surely a memorable one as it wound its way through the beautiful north Devon landscape.

After the 'Devon Belle' was withdrawn, the two observation cars were used by the Scottish

One of the preserved observation cars can now been seen on the Dartmouth Steam Railway in south Devon, while the other is on the Swanage Railway in Dorset.

Region for its Highland tours. Eventually No 13 found its way to the Dartmouth Steam Railway in south Devon, where it continues in regular service, while No 14 went to the USA in 1969 with the *Flying Scotsman* tour but was not immediately returned because of financial difficulties. It was finally tracked down to an office building in San Francisco and repatriated to the UK in 2007, where it was refurbished and officially returned to service on the Swanage Railway in Dorset on 16 July 2008.

Seaton Junction and the Seaton Tramway

Seaton Junction

Seaton Junction was not just a junction – it was also a station to board the branch-line train to Seaton, a small town on the south Devon coast on the estuary of the River Axe. The station was situated on the LSWR main line from London Waterloo to Exeter and opened for business on 19 July 1860 as 'Colyton for Seaton'. It was then renamed as 'Colyton Junction', and finally to 'Seaton Junction' in 1869.

During 1927/28 the station was reconstructed to enable the branch line to have its own dedicated platform on the south side, with sidings and access to the main running lines. The platform was set at an angle of 45 degrees to the main line to allow the branch to approach on an easy curve. Prior to the new platform, trains from Seaton went onto the main line, past the station, then reversed into the down platform, therefore shunting passengers 200 yards in reverse. This was considered to be unacceptable! The reconstruction also included two through tracks in the middle between the platform lines. This arrangement allowed through trains to pass at speed and definitely favoured westbound trains for Exeter, as Seaton

Tram No 12 is at one of the passing loops along the line. This tram was built in Eastbourne in 1966 and was originally single-deck, but was rebuilt in 1980 as a double-deck open-top, then modified again in 1999 to resemble the Feltham trams of the 1930s.

Seen here is Tram No 9, built in Bolton and Seaton and entering service in 2007, resembling both Plymouth and Blackburn trams.

Tram No 2 is just entering the yard at Seaton. It was built in 1964 at Eastbourne and is based on the London Metropolitan trams. The River Axe is directly to right of the picture.

Junction was at the bottom of Honiton Bank, which in the up direction presented a 6-mile (9.6km) climb at 1 in 80 to the summit. Slow trains sometimes stalled and required the assistance of a banking locomotive at the rear. However, there were occasions when a banking locomotive was not readily available and if the Seaton branch line tank locomotive was to hand it was an admirable stand-in. The branch locomotive also helped out with shunting milk wagons for the Express Diary located adjacent to the station on the up side.

Seaton Junction station was closed at the same time as the branch line on 7 March 1966.

Seaton branch line

The branch line itself was opened for traffic on 16 March 1868 and the LSWR ran the line, which was only 4¼ miles (6.8km) long and followed the attractive Axe Valley to Seaton Town station on the estuary of the River Axe. There were two intermediate stations between Seaton Town and the Junction at Colyton and Colyford. At that time, as a single-track line, it operated under the 'one engine in steam' system, so signalling was not an important issue, but

by 1899 the Tyer's electric tablet system was installed with a signal box at Colyton to enable more than one train on the line.

Various steam locomotives were used in the early years, but after the Second World War 'M7' 0-4-0 tank locomotives were the mainstay of the line, working in push-pull auto-train mode; however, towards the end GWR pannier tanks and GWR 0-4-2 tanks were frequently used. As the popularity of summer holidays became the norm, traffic on the line increased and by 1949 it was not unusual to see a nine-coach train with two locomotives. Seaton Town carriages were frequently added at Waterloo and uncoupled at Seaton Junction for onward travel down the branch line. But with the inevitable increase

A good view of Seaton Junction in 1961 shows a train from London Waterloo hauled by an unidentified rebuilt 'Merchant Navy' Class 4-6-2 just about to leave for Plymouth – the two white head codes indicate the Waterloo–Plymouth route. An unidentified loco with two carriages can be seen in the Seaton branch line platform.

in road transport and private cars, the through coaches from Waterloo onto the branch were withdrawn. By the early 1960s steam was replaced with DMUs, and by 7 March 1966 the branch line was sadly closed.

Seaton Electric Tramway

It was fortuitous that in 1969 the disused trackbed of the branch line was back in business, not with trains but with trams.

Claude Lane, whose hobby was rebuilding old trams to overall smaller sizes than the originals, was leasing two-thirds of a mile (1.06km) of 2-foot gauge (610mm) track at Eastbourne in East Sussex, and by 1956 had regauged the track to 2ft 9in (838mm). To increase the number of his trams and to run more, it was necessary to find a more appropriate place to relocate.

In 1969 he found and negotiated to buy the disused branch line from British Rail, the new track together with the necessary 120V DC electrical equipment was installed during 1969-71, and the trams were relocated to Seaton for conversion to the wider 2ft 9in (838mm) gauge.

Since the opening day, Colyton and Colyford stations have been made more tourist-friendly, and there are six passing loops to allow several trams on the 3-mile (4.8km) line to run in both directions. The line does not proceed further than Colyton, as Seaton Junction no longer exists.

At the Seaton Town end of the line the original station was demolished, and the purpose-built Edwardian-style terminal building, that was pleasing to the eye, is being replaced by a more

This is Seaton Junction today on the old Southern main line, which is now just a single track looking in the Honiton direction. The island platform for both the down main line and branch line is totally taken over by nature and there is little to show that the branch line existed. The station building to the right is now used by a commercial business.

An unidentified GWR 0-4-2T with one carriage in auto-train mode calls at Colyford station during a winter in the 1950s. Note the cast-iron gents toilet to the left with white painted tyres and box containing wallflowers for spring flowering. *Sue Bowman, Seaton Tramway*

At Colyton station in the late 1950s is GWR 0-6-0 pannier tank No 6430, built at Swindon in 1937 and withdrawn from service in 1964. *Sue Bowman, Seaton Tramway*

Rather neglected 0-4-2 GWR tank locomotive No 1442, hissing steam from everywhere, has just arrived at Seaton station with its one carriage in the early 1960s, shortly to return to Seaton Junction in auto-train mode. This locomotive was built in Swindon in 1935 and withdrawn in 1965; it now resides at Tiverton's Museum of Mid Devon. *Sue Bowman, Seaton Tramway*

modern undercover tramshed with cafe, gift shop and more. Currently there are approximately 12 operational trams. Unfortunately, Claude Lane suffered a fatal heart attack in April 1971, but the tramway has continued to thrive with its host of colourful trams. On 28 June 2018 the new terminus was opened at Seaton to provide a completely undercover experience for the increased number of tourists, providing four platforms, cafe and history areas.

Swanage Railway

There are quite a few successful heritage railways in the West of England, including the South Devon Railway, the Dartmouth Steam Railway, the Swanage Railway, the East Somerset Railway and the Bodmin & Wenford Railway, but it is not practical to expand on all of them here.

The Swanage line was a 9½-mile (15.3km) single-track standard-gauge branch line that opened in 1885 from an original station at Wareham on the London & South Western Railway (LSWR) Bournemouth-Weymouth main line to a terminus at Swanage on the Isle of Purbeck, just a short distance from the sea. Wareham station was replaced in 1887 with a larger, more functional building just a short distance away to handle both main-line and branch traffic. The branch left the main line at Worgret Junction, just over a mile west of Wareham station. At that time there were five mixed passenger and goods trains each way daily. There was substantial mineral traffic from ball clay mining and stone quarrying on Purbeck, but those companies used crude tramways for transportation to Wareham or Swanage, then by boat to their destinations.

Eventually the early 1900s saw an increase in holidaymakers to the area and a need to increase the number of trains. Also, the various mineral companies had, by then, rail connections to the branch line and to the rest of the railway network via transfer sidings at Furzebrook. In 1923 the LSWR was absorbed into the Southern Railway, and in 1948 became British Railways. The branch-line trains were then mainly operating in push-pull mode, and by 1969 steam had been replaced by BR Class 205 DMUs manufactured at Eastleigh. A review in 1967 showed the line to be unprofitable and was scheduled for closure, but managed to survive until 3 January 1972. The line from Furzebrook to Wareham remained operational for the transportation of ball clay and also, by then, crude oil from the small oilfield near Furzebrook.

May 1972 saw a start on bringing the line

Above right: At Swanage station in 1958 a train is ready to depart for Wareham, headed by Class 'M7' 0-4-4T No 30058, built in 1906 and withdrawn in 1960. Behind is an unidentified Maunsell-designed SR 2-6-0 'N' Class locomotive. *Mike Morant collection*

Right: A branch line train is ready to leave Wareham station in 1966 for the 10¼-mile (16.4km) picturesque trip to Swanage headed by grimy Class 2MT-A 2-6-2T No 41224. It was built at Crewe Works in 1948 and withdrawn from service in 1967. It spent its last years operating from Brighton shed. *Dr Neil Clifton*

Left: Resplendent Class 33 Bo-Bo diesel-electric No 33103 *Swordfish* is seen here in 2009 at Swanage station. It was built in 1960 by the Birmingham Railway Carriage & Wagon Company and had the original BR No 6514. These locos are commonly known as 'Cromptons', as their electrical equipment was supplied by Crompton Parkinson.

Centre: Having just run round and now coupled to its coaches, BR 4MT 2-6-4T No 80078 is ready to leave for Norden during 2009. It was built in 1954, withdrawn in 1965 and taken to Woodham Brothers' scrapyard, but was rescued and restored in 1976. It has been in the care of preservationists ever since.

Below: Eddystone is a fine example of SR designer Oliver Bulleid's rebuilt 'West Country' Class 4-6-2s. No 34028 (SR No 21C139) was built at Brighton Works in 1946 and withdrawn in 1964. Its original air-smoothed casing was removed and the locomotive rebuilt in 1957.

Almost ready for a return trip to Norden is 'bubble car' Class 121 No W55028, a double-ended single diesel unit, built by Pressed Steel Co in 1960. It was bought from Southwest Trains during 2009, with whom it had been utilised for driver route training.

back to life with the formation of the Swanage Railway Society, but BR was quick off the mark and started to lift the track, and Swanage Town Council started to demolish Swanage station. However, after much wrangling the Swanage Railway Society and Dorset County Council, which had acquired railway land, joined the new Southern Steam Trust to take the next step.

By 1979 a short length of line had been reopened and further extended in 1988, and by 1995 the line was opened for business between Swanage and Norden Park and Ride station, then finally connected to the existing Furzebrook freight line from Motala to Wareham in January 2002.

Today special trains can arrive from the national railway network, and make their way direct to Swanage station. It pays to be connected to the national network!

The Cornish clay industry

Kaolin or, as we know it, china clay, was discovered in Cornwall around 1760, and by the 1880s the china clay pits, mostly around St Austell, were owned and operated by the likes of Wedgwood, Spode and Minton, which were expanding rapidly in Staffordshire. However, as extraction became a more commercial business the pits were bought by adventurous companies.

A typical clayworks consisted of the pit, a waste tip, settling tanks, where the water removal process started, and finally the drying process. This was achieved in a long building known as a 'dry', with settling tanks at the back that fed onto the drying floor heated by a furnace underneath. The dried clay was then temporarily stored until shipment. For every ton of usable clay there is 5 tons of waste, and over the years the waste tips have grown into large white mounds locally known as the 'Cornish Alps'.

In parallel with china clay extraction, Cornwall was rich in copper, tin and iron, and the output of these mines together with the china clay needed to be transported away to other parts of the UK or to the continent.

In 1829 Joseph Thomas Treffry, known as the 'King of Mid Cornwall', built Par Harbour, 2 miles (3.2km) east of St Austell, a safe haven for up to 50 small sailing vessels. Charlestown, another harbour 3½ miles (5.6km) from St Austell, opened in 1801, but was much smaller in size than Par. A bigger problem was moving the clay from the pits to the harbours as extraction increased to meet the commercial needs, so a small narrow-gauge tramway fed into Charlestown with chutes strategically placed around the harbour walls for loading into the boats. Treffry built two horse-drawn tramways, one to Newquay on the north coast that was more convenient for some of his clay pits, and one to the south coast at Par.

On the south side the tramway from the pits around Bugle came through Luxulyan and down to Ponts Mill at the bottom of the Luxulyan Valley, where the clay was then transported by barge along a short stretch of canal to Par Harbour. On the return there was a major incline to a height of 325 feet (99 metres) above ground level. Treffry's answer was to build a combined viaduct and aqueduct across the valley where the tramway was laid on top and a waterway underneath. Water was readily available at the top, but on the wrong side of the valley, so it flowed through the viaduct and operated a water wheel to haul up the wagons from below. The excess water then flowed down the leat to Treffry's copper mine, Fowey

Top: This is *Alfred*, a standard-gauge 0-4-0ST built in 1953 by W. G. Bagnall for use in moving clay wagons around Par Harbour. *Alfred* and his counterpart *Judy* were of much reduced height to enable them to pass through a low tunnel under the main line. *Mike Morant collection*

Above: This is the picturesque harbour of Charlestown today, once a loading point for Cornish clay. In the foreground can be seen one of the chutes used for that purpose.

Consols, which made full use of the water.

By 1860 many of the horse-drawn tramways were being converted to standard-gauge railways and Treffry's tramways became the 46 miles (73.6km) of the Cornwall Minerals Railway with a main line from Newquay Harbour in the north to Fowey Harbour in the

The traverser at Fowey deep-water jetties has two tracks in and the two tracks out. The two inside tracks are for the forward traverser and the outer two for the rear traverser. On entering the shed, the steel wagons unload from the bottom and are then moved empty onto the traversers that move them sideways and out. *Craig Munday*

south, with branches off to Par Harbour and eventually to Padstow and Wenford Bridge. The Lostwithiel & Fowey Railway constructed a convenient junction at Lostwithiel, where there are still sidings in use for today's freight-only trains. Leaving Lostwithiel the short line runs along the side of the attractive Fowey River to the deep-water jetties at Carne Point, Fowey.

By 1919 English China Clays (ECC) was formed from three of the largest producers, but with over-production and falling demand more mergers were to follow in 1931 and 1954 with business interests in building, quarrying and transport. Finally, in 1999 the business was taken over by a French company, Imerys.

Today, Treffry's Newquay Harbour is no more, having closed in 1926, but the ex-GWR rail line is still in use for passengers. The rail branch between Fowey and Par was closed in 1968 and the track removed in favour of a concrete private road used by Imerys's trucks, which also use the 1173-yard (1,075-metre) Pinnock Tunnel at St Blazey, taking clay by road to Fowey Harbour. Charlestown Harbour is now a quaint and attractive tourist destination with its tall ships coming and going. The clay chutes and some of the narrow-gauge lines are still to be seen.

Par Harbour closed in 2007, as it could not accommodate large enough vessels, as most of the clay today is piped as bulk slurry into large ocean-going ships. The harbour had the distinction of owning two reduced-height steam locomotives named *Judy* and *Alfred*, built by W. J. Bagnall and delivered to Par in 1937 and 1953 respectively. The height restriction on the locos allowed them to pull wagons through the tunnel under the main line.

Fowey deep-water jetties are where clay shipment is centralised for shipment. Originally, the wagons, nicknamed 'hoods', were made of

On the traverser an empty wagon is moved to its exit track. *Craig Munday*

wood with the clay piled inside and protected by a tarpaulin pitch cover. Today they are steel bodied CDA hoppers of 32-ton capacity operated in block trains. The single line expands to four lines on entering the unloading area; there are two lines where the clay is emptied through the base of the wagons and traversers then move them sideways to the outgoing lines. The clay is then moved by a conveyer belt system to be loaded into the ships. There is a travelling bulk clay conveyer that traverses along the quay on fixed rails to fill ships' holds.

Left: A ship at the dock is being loaded from the bulk conveyor system from the wagon unloading shed.

Below: A rake of clay wagons is hauled towards Fowey by Class 66 No 66115, still showing EWS livery.

Rather battered Class 08 diesel locomotive No 08782, built in 1960 and named *Castleton Works* (with the 'T' missing), is used for shunting at Fowey.

This somewhat idyllic view from the Fowey River shows Class 66 No 66063 just leaving with a long rake of empty wagons.

This is Par Harbour around the beginning of the 20th century showing the extensive railway network and clay wagons in a siding waiting to be loaded on a boat. *Geof Sheppard collection*

The Treffry Viaduct near Luxulyan was a combined aqueduct and narrow-gauge tramway to transport the clay down to Par Harbour; the water turned a wheel at the bottom of the valley to haul the tramway wagons back to the top.

Ffestiniog Railway

The Ffestiniog Railway (FR) is the oldest independent railway company in the world still operating a train service, and is situated in a beautiful part of Wales on the edge of Snowdonia National Park.

In the beginning

The 1ft 11½ in (597mm) narrow-gauge line was opened in 1836 to transport slate from the quarries around Blaenau Ffestiniog, a small inland town 710 feet (216.4 metres) above sea level, to the coastal town of Porthmadog, a distance of about 13½ miles (21.6km). The slate was then loaded onto ships moored in the harbour, and exported around the globe as well as providing the needs of the home market. For the line to enter Porthmadog it had to cross The Cob, a man-made causeway opened in 1811 cut off the estuary of the River Glaslyn. The flow of the river was rerouted through sluice gates under the Britannia Bridge where the river now flows into Porthmadog Harbour. The Cob originally carried a road until the railway track was laid.

The railway was operated by gravity for the trip down to Porthmadog, and the empty slate wagons were hauled back to Blaenau by horses. The horses were carried on their trip back down in special 'dandy' wagons. The speed of descent was governed by the use of the natural contours, with cuttings and embankments being made to maintain an incline of about 1 in 80. Two brakemen were employed on each train to ensure that the downhill speed was properly controlled. To begin with a continuous run was not possible, as the Moelwyn Mountain got in the way and wagons went over the top via an incline until a tunnel was completed in 1844. It took about 1½ hrs to descend and 6 hours for the horses to pull eight empty wagons back up to the quarry terminus.

A timetable was published in 1856 by Charles Easton Spooner, Manager and Clerk to the Company, which allowed for six trains daily in each direction. It is known that from 1850 passengers were also carried, unofficially, and, of course, at their own risk.

This atmospheric view of Porthmadog is looking north towards Snowdonia. On the right the River Glaslyn can be seen meandering past The Cob towards the tidal sluice and the harbour.

Steam locomotives

By 1863 steam locomotives were introduced so that longer slate trains could be hauled up to Blaenau, but they continued to run downhill by gravity. Steam also allowed the official introduction of a passenger service from 1856, and the Ffestiniog became the first narrow-gauge railway in the UK to carry passengers using small, low-slung, four-wheeled coaches.

Top left: The Ffestiniog Railway crest. The origin of the design is not known, but note the spelling of Ffestiniog with only one 'F', as it was spelled the English way when cited in the Act of Parliament at its creation in 1832. Above the crest are the coronet and feathers of the Prince of Wales, which the railway has permission to use.

Top right: A wide-angle view shows Porthmadog Harbour station at a quiet period in the day. Opened to passengers in 1865 and built in local stone with Welsh slate roofs, it is the Head Office and Operational Headquarters of the Ffestiniog Railway.

Above right: This is the FR's 'double Fairlie' 0-4-4-0T No 10 *Merddin Emrys*, built at Boston Lodge in 1879. Looking immaculate, it is ready to leave Porthmadog to make its way over The Cob, then start its ascent to Blaenau Ffestiniog.

Right: Friendly helping hands are always available to keep the rolling stock clean. I told you to close the window!

Right: Locomotive No 14 *Lyd* is a 2-6-2T built in 2010 at Boston Lodge Works in the style of the locomotives of the old Lynton & Barnstaple Railway, and painted in Southern Railway livery. It is seen here assembling its coaches for the journey to Blaenau.

Centre right: A train has just left Porthmadog Harbour station and is making its way over The Cob towards Boston Lodge Works, situated on the bend, then upwards to Blaenau. The River Glaslyn is to the left and the Atlantic Ocean to the right.

Bottom right: A siding next to the main line by Minffordd yard contains slate wagons that are no longer used for that purpose except for demonstration purposes. On occasions a number of slate wagons, with slate, are formed into a train and run down from Blaenau to Porthmadog under gravity, as was the case in the 19th century.

The early locomotives were 0-4-0TTs and 0-4-4-0Ts, where T signifies a tank locomotive and TT a tank loco with a tender. Some of these first 0-4-0TT locomotives are still operational on the Ffestiniog. The 0-4-4-0Ts were of the more powerful, articulated, double-ended Fairlie design and have become synonymous with the Ffestiniog Railway today.

The bad times

With the advent of more modern roofing materials, the main use for Welsh slate started to decline and the FR's financial position was severely weakened. In 1921 a controlling interest was bought by the local Aluminium Corporation and the owner, a Mr Jack, became Chairman of the FR. He was also Chairman of the fledgling Welsh Highland Railway

(WHR). Both railways were to be managed from Porthmadog with maintenance carried out at the Boston Lodge Works at the far end of The Cob.

In 1923 Lt Col H. F. Stephens, of light railway fame, was appointed as part-time Engineer to both the FR and the WHR, and in 1925 became Chairman and Managing Director of both companies with a salary of £400 per year, with all administration being handled from his Tonbridge (Kent) offices. His efforts, as an Englishman, to cut costs and improve efficiency were not met with enthusiasm by the Welsh staff. The loss of the Moel Tryfan slate contract with the WHR, the prevailing economic conditions, and the preference of passengers to use buses, ended with the complete closure of the WHR in 1937. Stephens remained with the FR as its Chairman and Managing Director and Receiver and Manager of the WHR until his death in October 1931.

The FR passenger services, which relied heavily on tourism, ceased at the outbreak of war in September 1939 and the declining slate traffic managed to survive until 1946, when all operations came to an end. Nature then took over and the line soon became unusable.

In preservation

In 1951 the railway was sold to Mr Alan Pegler, a rail enthusiast, who intended to restore the line to a workable condition. By 1954

Top left: A ballast hopper in Minffordd yard feeds into small wagons for transportation to where track maintenance is being carried out.

Centre left: Earl of Merioneth, another double-ended Fairlie, pulls hard as the train rounds the curve approaching Dduallt Halt. It was from this point on the curve that the original line continued to the right and into the old Moelwyn Tunnel towards Tanygrisiau.

Left: Looking towards Blaenau from the new line, the old line can be seen in the centre of the photo ending abruptly at the edge of the reservoir.

the Ffestiniog Railway Trust had been formed and restoration continued, but the Central Electricity Generating Board (CEGB) had made a decision to build an electricity generating plant using a new reservoir and pumping station. Unfortunately, the rising waters of the Tanygrisiau reservoir flooded the adjacent track and the Moelwyn Tunnel, so a new way around was required. This resulted in the Lyn Ystradau Deviation, a rising loop, where the line went around and over itself, being raised well above the reservoir and through a new Moelwyn Tunnel. The work was carried out largely by volunteers between 1965 and 1977. During this

Above: The double-ended Fairlie *Earl of Merioneth*, No 11, waits to leave Blaenau with a train to Porthmadog. This is another 0-4-4-0T locomotive built at Boston Lodge Works in 1979 and the first 'double Fairlie' to be built by the restored Ffestiniog Railway.

Left: A view of Boston Lodge Works early in the morning. Locomotives are cleaned and the brass is being polished. After being fired and watered they will be coupled to their coaches for the day's work.

period trains were run at various times from Porthmadog to various points towards Blaenau. A new joint station at Blaenau for the FR and British Rail (formerly the old Great Western station) was eventually opened in 1982 and the FR could then carry passengers along the whole route from Porthmadog to Blaenau Ffestiniog.

The Ffestiniog Railway today

The Harbour station in Porthmadog is Victorian-built in the typical Welsh style, using local stone and of course a slate roof. It boasts a good cafe and bar named after Charles Spooner.

There is always plenty of activity around the station, especially in the tourist season, with carriage stock being shunted into position at the departure platform and immaculate 0-4-4-0T 'double Fairlie' locomotives waiting patiently to couple up to their coaches.

Leaving the Harbour station, trains accelerate across The Cob towards Boston Lodge Works at the end, where the running line turns sharply left towards Minffordd station at 85 feet (26 metres) above sea level. Minffordd is also where the track maintenance yard is situated and is accessed by a siding running back from the station. Before the siding turns right into the yard it passes the old weigh-house where the loaded slate trains passed over weighbridges before continuing to Porthmadog or into the yard. In the early days this was the exchange area between the FR slate wagons and Great Western Railway (GWR) for most of the slate destined for UK use. There were four GWR sidings that came off a long loop on the Cambrian main line, which still runs around the outside of the yard with a single station platform just below the FR's Minffordd station.

Minffordd yard is full of everything to keep the track and infrastructure in good running condition, such as sleepers, ground frames, wagons and vans for permanent way staff, rail-mounted cranes, a heavy lifting hoist and slate wagons used for track ballast. The ballast is loaded from an incline above into wagons about 8 feet (2.4 metres) below.

From Minffordd the line continues to follow the Vale of Ffestiniog, rising all the time towards Tan-y-Bwlch station at 430 feet (131 metres), where there is a passing loop and a platform between the two tracks. The next point of great interest has to be the Deviation at Dduallt, 540 feet (165 metres), where the track describes a complete circle, running over itself at Rhoslyn Bridge, giving a height gain of 35 feet (10.6 metres) to avoid the waters of the Tanygrisiau reservoir. The original line and old Moelwyn Tunnel can still be seen from the train.

At Tanygrisiau station, 640 feet (195 metres), there is another passing loop and the train is only 1½ miles (2.4km) from its destination, Blaenau Ffestiniog. At this point in the journey the grey mountains of slate and the increasing sparseness of forestation close in.

At Blaenau Ffestiniog station the narrow-gauge trains share the station with the standard-gauge Conwy Valley Line (Arriva Trains, Wales) from Llandudno. The Ffestiniog Railway has its own low-level island platform with a footbridge over the Conwy Valley Line, which is also the entrance to and exit from the town. The locomotives then uncouple, run round on the loop to couple up, and take their trains back down to Porthmadog.

The all-important younger volunteers are putting in some elbow grease to make *Lyd* shine, under the watchful eye of a man who knows!

Vans Nos 6 and 7 stand in a siding at Boston Lodge. They were both built there: No 6 in 1856 as a quarrymen's 3rd Class coach, and No 7 in 1898.

Locomotives and rolling stock

The railway has an interesting selection of approximately 13 steam locomotives, of which some are serviceable and others at varying stages of overhaul and maintenance. There are also a number of diesel locomotives from small Hunslet-type shunters to *Vale of Ffestiniog*,

a 335hp turbocharged B-B diesel-hydraulic built in South Africa for a Namibian diamond mine, finishing up at a cement works in Port Elizabeth. It was purchased by the FR in 1993 together with its twin, *Caernarfon Castle*, which operates on the Welsh Highland Line.

Boston Lodge Works

Boston Lodge is where steam and diesel locomotives, coaches and other rolling stock are restored, designed, built and lovingly maintained to keep both the Ffestiniog Railway and Welsh Highland Railway running smoothly. The works' reputation for fine engineering is highly regarded both at home and abroad.

A continuous supply of coal is required to keep the steam locomotives fed, which is delivered to Boston Lodge by the coal train from Minffordd yard, consisting of a rake of three ex-South African Railways all-steel, high-sided 'B wagons' hauled by a diesel locomotive like *Criccieth Castle*, an 0-6-0 built in 1995 at Boston Lodge.

The morning's work gets under way inside Boston Lodge Works. The railway has everything here to build, repair and maintain the locomotives and rolling stock.

The regular coal train arrives from Minffordd yard, providing the necessary fuel for the locomotives. In charge of the train is an 0-6-0 diesel named *Criccieth Castle*, built in 1995 at Boston Lodge with parts supplied by Baguley-Drewry.

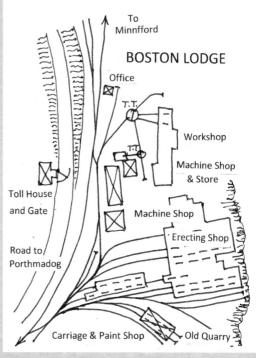

BOSTON LODGE

To Minnfford

Office

T.T.

Workshop

Machine Shop & Store

Toll House and Gate

Machine Shop

Road to Porthmadog

Erecting Shop

Carriage & Paint Shop

Old Quarry

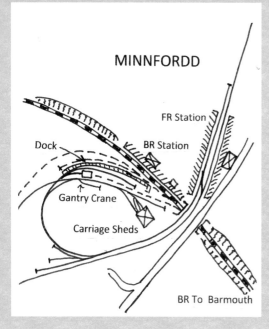

MINNFORDD

FR Station

Dock

BR Station

Gantry Crane

Carriage Sheds

BR To Barmouth

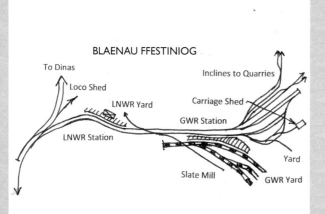

BLAENAU FFESTINIOG

To Dinas

Loco Shed

Inclines to Quarries

LNWR Yard

Carriage Shed

GWR Station

LNWR Station

Yard

Slate Mill

GWR Yard

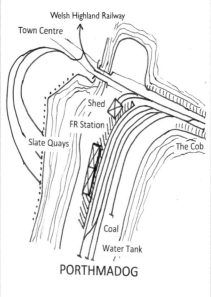

Welsh Highland Railway

Town Centre

Shed

FR Station

Slate Quays

The Cob

Coal

Water Tank

PORTHMADOG

Welsh Highland Railway

The Welsh Highland Railway (WHR) had been closed down since 1937, but in 1990 the FR took on the commitment to rebuild and open the line using 1ft 11½in (597mm) narrow-gauge track in uniformity with the FR. The line is 25 miles (40.2km) from Caernarfon to Porthmadog Harbour station. The first section from Caernarfon to Dinas was opened and operated by the FR in October 1997. The original line started at Dinas, which was the junction with the London & North Western Railway (LNWR) standard-gauge line between Caernarfon and Afonwen, near Pwllheli. The WHR built the new Dinas-Caernarfon extension on the original trackbed under a Light Railway Order. Various legal procedures hampered the restoration of the remaining route, and Porthmadog was not reached until 2010.

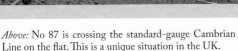

Above: No 87 is crossing the standard-gauge Cambrian Line on the flat. This is a unique situation in the UK.

Above: No 87, an ex-South African Railways Class 'NGC16' 2-6-2+2-6-2, was built in 1937 by Cockerill, and is seen here at the northern terminus of Caernarfon. The train has just arrived and the loco will then run round to take the train back to Porthmadog, where the WHR shares the station with the Ffestiniog.

Left: This is No 143, another ex-South African Railways 'NGC16' 2-6-2+2-6-2 built in 1950 by Beyer Peacock of Manchester. It is seen here crossing the Glaslyn River as the line runs through the rugged and spectacular Aberglaslyn Pass.

No 87 leaves Porthmadog Harbour station and weaves across the main street and over the Glaslyn River; it will then turn right to make its way towards Caernarfon. On the outskirts of Porthmadog the narrow-gauge line crosses the standard-gauge Cambrian Line.

Rolling stock

As the WHR gauge is the same as the FR, much of the stock is interchangeable and locomotives are maintained from Boston Lodge Works, although stabling and maintenance is also carried out at Dinas. The WHR does have its own coal-fired locomotives that work the line regularly, and are ex-Tasmanian Government Railways and South African Railways Garratts built by Beyer Peacock of Manchester and John Cockerill in Belgium. There are three currently in service, a 'K' Class 0-4-0+0-4-0, and two 'NGG16' Class 2-6-2+2-6-2s.

These locomotives, named after the designer Herbert William Garratt, are articulated and consist of three separate frames, as opposed to a normal single-frame locomotive. The power units and running gear are at the front and rear sections, which also carry water and coal, with the central frame for the boiler and cab connected to the power units by pivoting joints. Although they are long and powerful locomotives, their articulation enables them to negotiate the tight curves that are usually associated with narrow-gauge lines.

Signalling

There are no signals on the WHR. which uses the traditional Staff and Ticket system where the section token staff or a numbered ticket is issued to the train for single-line operation; if just one train is in operation on the line the train crew use the token only, but if more than one train is in operation in the same direction, numbered tickets are issued to allow trains to pass through each section, the last train taking the token staff. When the train reaches its destination the token staff is then used to allow the return of another train or trains.

It is hoped that this arrangement can be replaced with the more modern Electronic Token System (ETS) in the future.

Caernarfon

Caernarfon WHR station is situated on the trackbed of the old LNWR line across the car park from Caernarfon Castle. The current station building is a temporary-looking affair and is separate from the single platform. As the single track enters the station it splits into a run-round loop with the track terminating at a buffer stop about 50 yards (46 metres) past the platform end. Both platform and tracks are restricted by a very high stone wall beside the tracks and a stone wall on the platform side separating them from the adjacent road. Welsh Government funding has helped to build new station, car and coach park, which was completed during 2018/19.

From Caernarfon the WHR line travels through some of the most beautiful and dramatic scenery that Snowdonia has to offer, especially where the line crosses the Glaslyn River and runs through the Aberglaslyn Pass just a few feet away from the shallow, fast-flowing waters.

Porthmadog Harbour station

The track runs into the outskirts of Porthmadog, over the unique flat crossing of the standard-gauge Cambrian Line (Machynlleth to Pwllheli), then along the side of the Glaslyn River to the Britannia Bridge. The line then turns sharply over the road bridge (High Street) and into the Harbour station yard. Traffic is halted by flashing signals and a siren until the train clears the High Street. It's certainly different!

WELSH HIGHLAND & FFESTINIOG RAILWAYS

SNOWDONIA NATIONAL PARK

To Caernavon
Waenfawr
Dinas Junction
Bettws Garmon
Quellyn Lake
South Snowdon
Pitts Head
Hafod Ruffyd
Beddgelert
Abrgalslyn
Hafod Garregog
Ynysfor
Pont Creosor
GWR
Porthmadog
To Criceeth
Boston
Lodge
CAERNARFON BAY

LNWR LMSR
LNWR
Blaenau Ffestiniog
GWR
Tanymanod
Tyddyngwyn
Tany Greisia
Teigl Halt
Moelwyn
Llan Festiniog
Ddualt
Tan-y-Bwlch
Penrhyn
Deudrath
Minnfford
GWR
Maentwrog Road
Talsarnau
GWR
To Bala

Until recently WHR trains arriving at Harbour station caused operation difficulties integrating with the Ffestiniog trains. To overcome these the Harbour station and The Cob have undergone major construction works to enable the WHR trains and FR trains to operate simultaneously by adding a new island platform and run-round loop for the WHR. To achieve this The Cob has been widened at the station end to accommodate the new platform together with the installation of new track, points, signals, signal box and relay room.

Penmaenmawr quarries

The Snowdonia National Park in North Wales is an area of spectacular scenery, with mountains, lakes, rivers and forests, but is also a source of slate and granite.

Situated on the north-western edge of the park, where the mountains come down to the seashore of Conwy Bay, is the Penmaenmawr Granite Quarry. Penmaenmawr literally means Great Stone Head, but continuous quarrying has now reduced the mountain to a hill!

The quarry opened for business in 1830 under the partnership of Dennis Brundrit and Philip Whiteway, and during the early days scree boulders were found at lower levels and were transported out to small coastal vessels using a timber-built pier, as roads were totally inadequate for transporting heavy materials. As time went by, and to regularise this arrangement, a Crown Lease was applied for and granted, allowing them to gradually remove areas of the mountain, together with the opening of new quarrying areas and the building of another pier. The granite was lowered from the quarries by self-acting inclines to a 3-foot (914mm) narrow-gauge railway that transported the granite to the pier heads for loading on to the boats. Other partnerships also opened quarries and inclines and built their own piers.

Between 1845 and 1847 the Chester to Holyhead railway was constructed and later became part of the London & North Western Railway's (LNWR) coastal main line, which ran between the quarries and the seashore. Interconnecting narrow-gauge networks sped up production and transfer sidings were constructed to unload the narrow-gauge wagons into standard-gauge private-owner wagons for onward travel by the LNWR. The first train of railway ballast was despatched on 15 August 1889 using 20-ton wooden ballast wagons, with one or two trains leaving every day.

In 1911 the two quarry businesses of Brindrit and Darbishire amalgamated to form the Penmaenmawr & Welsh Granite Co Ltd, and

In this view across the bay towards Great Orme Head, the London & North Western Railway main line can be seen in the foreground with the Brundrit & Co Ltd private sidings just beyond, with their own standard-gauge wagons in situ for loading. The stone is loaded from the side-tipping narrow-gauge wagons on the raised platform. *Penmaenmawr Historical Society*

This unusual view from Caernarfon Bay shows the coaster *Puffin* left high and dry at low water, being loaded with stone. A series of double inclines for use by the narrow-gauge wagons can be seen climbing the hill to connect with a mill on the right. Note the enormous amount of spoil-tip scree that reaches down to the houses. *Penmaenmawr Historical Society*

set about modernising the two main shipping piers to speed up loading with large concrete hoppers and chutes. In 1931 modernisation continued with construction of a standard-gauge system to transport the granite to a new primary crusher using two Avonside-built diesel locomotives, Nos 2062 and 2063, named *Kimberley* and *Alice*. In 1933 an ex-London Midland & Scottish Railway (LMS) 0-4-0T locomotive, No 11245, was purchased. These locomotives worked at the higher level and were initially hauled up the inclines on specially manufactured trolleys.

On the narrow-gauge network Motor Rail diesels were used together with locally built De Winton locomotives with distinctive vertical boilers, several Hunslet 0-4-0ST locomotives, an Armstrong Whitworth 0-4-0 diesel, and two Ruston Hornsby four-wheel diesels.

By the 1950s several of the rail inclines had been replaced by conveyor belts, hastening the demise of the narrow-gauge network, which

At Darbishire's granite quarry and Braichlwyd Mill, a narrow-gauge locomotive is sitting outside the shed with three side-tipping wagons. The locomotive is thought to be a Hunslet named *Hughie*. To the right of the shed is a De Winton 0-4-0 with a vertical boiler trundling along with some wagons. *Penmaenmawr Historical Society*

This view of Penmarian Mill at Darbishire & Co Ltd's granite quarry shows the steep inclines serving the lower levels. A wagon turntable can be seen in the foreground as space was restricted on the side of the mountain.
Penmaenmawr Historical Society

One of the local De Winton vertical boiler 0-4-0 locomotives named *Llanfair* is seen here out of use and gradually rusting away, although signs of the old livery and double coach lining are just visible. *Penmaenmawr Historical Society*

was finally closed down in 1965.

By the 1980s the business had seen a succession of owners, which all eventually merged to become ARC (Amey Roadstone Corporation), which made some improvements including a new rail wagon loader with larger storage hoppers holding 5,000 tonnes of stone.

The standard-gauge quarry sidings were also realigned to accommodate the dualling of the busy A55 coast road that runs between the railway and the shoreline.

Hanson then took over the aggregate business, but at the end of 2008 had lost its contract to supply Network Rail with ballast and announced that it was to mothball the quarrying works at Penmaenmawr, but would keep the concrete and asphalt plants in production.

Above left: A narrow-gauge Hunslet 0-4-0 diesel, Works No HE 3129, was delivered new to Penmaenmawr in October 1944. It had a four-cylinder McLaren 80hp engine fitted with Westinghouse air brakes and was named *Vixen*. It is seen here in June 1968 hauling some wooden side-tipping wagons. A number of upended disused wagons are in the foreground. *Penmaenmawr Historical Society*

Above right: The narrow-gauge Hunslet 0-4-0 No 206, built in 1899 and named *Hughie*, was delivered to Darbishire & Co in January 1900. It was in dark green livery with black and white lining, with an underframe in black and red lining and red buffer beams. It fell out of use in 1942 and was eventually scrapped in 1951.

A later scene in the 1980s shows four private sidings of Amey Roadstone Construction (Northern) Ltd and the rail loading plant and storage silos that occupy a narrow stretch of land between the quarries and the A55 coastal road. The Conwy, Bangor and Holyhead main line is squeezed in between the A55 and the shoreline. Class 37 No 37109, built around 1960 by English Electric, shunts an assortment of steel two-axle bogie and hopper ballast wagons. *Hanson Aggregates*

The WLLR's No 2 locomotive, No 823 *Countess* in GWR green livery, heads a mixed freight train for Llanfair approaching Cyfronydd in October 2018. Like *The Earl* it was built by Beyer Peacock in 1902 at the company's Gorton Works in Manchester with GWR/BR number 823, and ran on the line from 1903 until closure. *Andrew Frewster*

Welshpool & Llanfair Light Railway

Most of the narrow-gauge railways in Wales were constructed to bring slate and aggregates to the west coast ports for transhipment to customers worldwide. There were a few exceptions built for the increasing tourist trade, but one unique and isolated inland line was constructed for developing the agriculture in the border county of Montgomeryshire, utilising the Light Railways Act of 14 August 1896.

Work on the 2ft 6in (762mm)-gauge Welshpool & Llanfair Light Railway (WLLR) commenced on 30 May 1901, the contractor being John Strachan of Cardiff. Under the Light Railway Order, the rails were 45lb to a yard, flat-bottomed in 30-foot lengths, spiked to sleepers, and with check rails for sharp curves and the Golfa Bank gradient and bridges. Speed was limited to 20mph, which gave a journey time of 55 minutes each way between Welshpool

and Llanfair Caereinion. The line commenced with interchange facilities with the Cambrian Railways at Welshpool and ran due west into the hills, terminating at Llanfair Caereinion, a distance of 9 miles 88 yards (14.56km). The line runs south of the A458 road and crosses the River Banwy several times, including a stream in a back street in the middle of Welshpool. At the WLLR yard there was a transhipment shed and a dual-gauge siding to the north side of the Cambrian and WLLR goods yard. As livestock was an important commodity, two cattle and sheep docks were provided. A joint WLLR carriage and engine shed provided a covered service area.

The Board of Trade sanctioned the opening on 4 March 1903, with the first passenger train service on 4 April using two 0-6-0 tank engines named *The Earl* and *The Countess* built by Beyer Peacock of Manchester and delivered during September 1902. In 1923 the Cambrian Railways and Welshpool & Llanfair Railway were amalgamated into the Great Western Railway (GWR). Both locos were sent to

No 823 *Countess* is seen again having her water level checked before continuing on to Llanfair with its mixed freight train. *Andrew Frewster*

Swindon in 1929 and were returned with their new GWR 'Westernisation' look. They now sported new copper-capped chimneys, top water feed, large steam domes and brass trumpet safety valve covers, which adorned the new boilers.

Under the auspices of the Cambrian Railways the company had maintained and run the railway, and compensation was paid to the WLLR at the time of absorption. The GWR ran three mixed trains each way daily together with specials for fetes and agricultural shows. Freight traffic of coal and minerals was the prime business, supported by milk and agricultural products and livestock. The Standard Quarry supplied a small trade, as did timber traffic to Welshpool; the latter was restricted to 10mph because of the weight on the bogie-bolster wagons. While the farmers waited for the arrival of the freight trains at Llanfair, they evidently propped up the Home-Brew bar at the Wynnstay Arms Hotel. The local lime and coal merchant at Llanfair was J. Lloyd Peate & Sons, which unusually had five private-owner 10-ton open wagons painted in maroon with white letters. This is believed to be a unique situation where private-owner wagons were used on the Welsh narrow-gauge, other than those used for internal use only.

Rolling stock from the outset consisted of three coaches, 40 open wagons, four covered vans, two cattle vans, and two brake vans. R. Y. Pickering of Wishaw provided these, as well as the five private-owner wagons together with sheep wagons and the timber bogie bolster wagons.

As the attraction of road transport became apparent, the railway business gradually slipped away to road haulage companies and buses. The last freight train, which was then under British Railways ownership, ran on 2 November 1956 and the last passenger train left Welshpool on Saturday 7 February 1960.

As with several other Welsh narrow-gauge railways, enthusiastic preservationists took upon themselves the hard work of reopening the WLLR. On 4 January 1960 the Welshpool & Llanfair Light Railway Preservation Company Ltd was incorporated. This attractive railway was officially reopened on Saturday 8 April 1963 and has enjoyed continued success to the present day. Four additional coaches were acquired from the Admiralty railway at Upnor, Kent, whose last train ran on 29 May 1961. Austrian coaches with end balconies came from the renowned Zillertalbahn in 1968. Since that date several locomotives have been added to the two originals.

The WLLR's No1 locomotive, *The Earl* (GWR/BR number 822), chugs towards Cyfronydd through the lush Montgomeryshire countryside with a mixed freight train for Llanfair. *Andrew Frewster*

These are:

Upnor Castle 4wd built by Hibberd in 1951 (Admiralty)
Monarch 0-4-4-0T Bagnall of 1953
Nutty 0-4-0 vertical boiler Sentinel of 1929
Chattenden 0-6-0d Baguley of 1949
Wynnstay 0-6-0d Fowler of 1951 (from Sierra Leone)

Sir Dreyaldwyn 0-8-0T Franco/Belge of 1944 (German military use)
Raven 0-4-0d Hunslet of 1934
Joan 0-6-2T Kerr Stuart of 1927 (West Indies)

This wide selection of home-grown locos and a 'foreigner' also includes ex-MOD locos.

The Earl is seen here on shunting duties just outside the station at Llanfair. *Countess* can be seen inside the loco shed to the right. The line to Welshpool runs past the shed and into the distance. *Andrew Frewster*

Top left: An example of one of the other locomotives is this 1949 0-6-0 diesel locomotive No 7 *Chattenden*. It was built by E. E. Baguley of Burton-on-Trent to the order of the Drewry Car Co Ltd and was originally employed by the Admiralty on the Upnor & Lodge Railway, opposite Chatham on the River Medway in Kent. It has been at the WLLR since 1968.

Top right: The Earl is seen here at Llanfair ready to leave with four carriages for Welshpool. The two rear carriages are ex-Hungarian and the front two are ex-Austrian Zillertalbahn.

Above: The passenger train for Welshpool pulls away from Llanfair station with *The Earl*, looking in perfect condition, leading the way.

At Wharf station at Towyn in 1952 is a split-screen 'Corona' lorry delivering soft drinks, with *Dolgoch* and her two coaches and ticket van about to leave for Towyn Pendre station.

Talyllyn Railway

The natural wealth of Wales is in the hills where the world's best-quality roofing slates are quarried. These small inland quarries in mountainous areas initially transported the slates by horseback to the coast where they were loaded onto coastal sailing ships. As demand grew, so it became necessary for a speedier form of transport, and the several Welsh narrow-gauge railways were born.

The Ffestiniog was the leader in this enterprise, with James Spooner its engineer, designing the exceptional gravity-worked railway from the quarries at Blaenau Ffestiniog to Porthmadog harbour in 1836. In 1863, soon after James's death, Charles, his younger son, introduced steam locomotives. The McConnel family, who owned the Bryn Eglwys quarries, proposed a similar railway to Aberdovey and appointed Charles's elder brother, James Swinton Spooner, as engineer. The plans had included a line from Towyn to Aberdovey, but they were pipped at the post by the promotion of the Aberystwyth & Welsh Coast Railway, so

they reduced their narrow-gauge railway to the 6½ miles from Abergynolwyn to Towyn.

An Act of Authorisation stipulated that the gauge should be not more than standard nor less than 2ft 3in. This was the gauge chosen, probably because the nearby Corris Railway was already operating using that gauge. Inspection of the line on 8 September 1866 by Captain H. W. Tyler, raised concern regarding its only passenger coach, whose width of 5ft 3in meant that there was only 1ft 11in between the coach side and bridge abutments instead of the required 2ft 6in. To overcome this problem it was resolved that on one side only the doors and windows would be locked and the track slewed over where required so as to comply with the Board of Trade regulations – no looking out of windows for photography on that side! The Talyllyn is unique in this respect. Another unique feature of its rolling stock is a brake van with two sliding doors and a built-in travelling ticket office and serving hatch!

The line was opened for slate traffic in 1865 and for passengers on 1 October 1866, a distance of 6½ miles with a journey time of

45 minutes, travelling at around 10mph. The steepest gradients are 1 in 60 and there is only one major engineering feature, the Dolgoch Viaduct, 51 feet high and 38 yards long with three arches, built of local stone. The track consisted of both flat-bottomed rails, 21 feet long and of 44lb per linear yard with no fishplates, and some chaired rails. A mineral extension continued on from the Abergynolwyn station winding around an escarpment up the valley to the Bryn Eglwys quarries and the workmen's cottages. Here there were two inclines of 140 feet powered by water; sidings also reached into the village so that supplies could be delivered. 'One engine in steam' was the normal practice, with the locomotive facing uphill from Towyn Wharf station. There was no signalling. At Towyn Wharf station there were five tracks fanning out across the slate stock yard, which terminated at the interchange raised platform with the standard-gauge siding; this was later owned by the Cambrian Railways, then the GWR. A single-storey building was adequate for most administration purposes

The new Talyllyn Railway was supplied with two steam locomotives built by Fletcher Jennings & Co, Lowca Works, Whitehaven, Cumbria. The first delivered was No 1 *Talyllyn* in the autumn of 1865, and No 2 *Dolgoch* arrived a year later; both were built as 0-4-0s and without any form of protection for the driver. The first four-wheeled passenger coach was supplied by the Lancaster Wagon Works, with a further three similar coaches built by Brown, Marshall of Birmingham. All were four-wheelers, as is the brake-van-cum-ticket-office.

Half a mile inland from the Wharf station, at Towyn Pendre, next to the main line, were

Dolgoch, seen again at Towyn in 1952, was an 0-4-0T locomotive built by Fletcher Jennings in 1866 for the Talyllyn Railway, and has rear and well water tanks, an unusual feature.

Abergynolwyn's terminus station once had a rough track that led off to the Bryn Eglwys slate quarries. Seen here is *Edward Thomas*, an 0-4-2 saddle tank built by Kerr Stuart & Co Ltd in 1921 for the Corris Railway, and acquired by the TR in 1951.

five sidings, a long carriage shed, engine shed and workshops with inspection pits. The lathes, drilling machines, etc, were powered by a Hornsby horizontal engine, circa 1910, using transfer shafts and belts.

Backing onto the engine shed was a cottage for the level crossing keeper who looked after the

Edward Thomas runs between Rhydyronen and Abergynolwyn in the Afon Fathew valley, and will soon be crossing the viaduct at Dolgoch.

gates of the only road crossing on the railway. In later years this was occupied by a grand old gentleman, Peter Williams, distinguished by his flamboyant white moustache. He was a fountain of knowledge and was of immense help in the early days of preservation of the railway.

By 1946 the quarry was no longer producing slate and closed, leaving the railway completely bereft of income except for carrying a few passengers. The little railway was already running down with only one locomotive, *Dolgoch*, in working condition. The track was becoming dangerous through lack of maintenance and nature was beginning to take over.

The end came in October 1950 when the last train ran and the line finally closed forever.

But, that wasn't to be the case. Some preservationists headed by the renowned author, Tom Rolt, managed to have the shares transferred to a new society and work began in earnest to rebuild the railway.

The first train to be run by the Talyllyn Railway Preservation Society was on Monday 4 June 1951, and 15,000 passengers were carried in this first season. Much hard work gradually began to pay dividends, especially at Pendre yard where a new stone-built tower housed a water tank that supplied two tracks, and the level crossing gates were painted white and emblazoned with two red discs. At Towyn Wharf station there had been some track rationalisation with a buffer stop for the new platform track terminating at the interchange platform. The new passenger platform was later given a canopy roof, as was a two-storey building housing a superb museum opened in 2005 by the Prince of Wales and the Duchess of Cornwall. At Dolgoch Halt, close to the viaduct and waterfalls, which are a major attraction, the spring-fed water tower was renovated complete with its wooden troughs, one at high level supplying the water tank and another portable one housed under the tank to supply the locomotives. The halt is surrounded by rhododendrons and, with the high hills as a back drop, is a really delightful setting. To keep the passengers amused and the driver alert, there are regular intrusions by stray sheep enjoying the trackside grasses.

Rolling stock today includes a variety of 22 passenger coaches and goods wagons including several covered vans, based on the line's original 115 slate wagons. Coaches are painted red with varnished wood framing and locomotives are painted in several liveries. There are five varied diesel locomotives and six steam locomotives.

Above: On a sunny day at Towyn Wharf in 2005, 0-4-2T No 7 *Tom Rolt* pulls away towards Abergynolwyn. This locomotive was built at the Talyllyn's Pendre Works and came into service in 1991. *Simon Robinson*

Below right: Looking superb with its rake of equally well-turned-out coaches at Towyn Wharf in 2005 is locomotive No 4 *Edward Thomas*, waiting to start a day's work. *Simon Robinson*

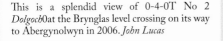

This is a splendid view of 0-4-0T No 2 *Dolgoch* at the Brynglas level crossing on its way to Abergynolwyn in 2006. *John Lucas*

Pendre station and workshops on the Talyllyn Railway, the world's first preserved railway, in the early 1950s.

Narrow gauge supreme! 0-4-0ST *Dolgoch* is named after the waterfalls at this station. It was built by Fletcher Jennings in 1864 and is still at work!

This is a large area covering Essex, Suffolk, Norfolk, Cambridgeshire, Bedfordshire and the Midlands, and is served from London by Fenchurch Street, Liverpool Street, Euston, King's Cross, St Pancras and Marylebone stations. On the eastern side Southend in Essex has always been popular with London daytrippers, while Norfolk, although mainly flat, has always attracted people for both boating holidays on the Broads and of course the sandy beaches of the east coast. Cambridgeshire is similarly flat and both counties have been ideal for chalk and silica sand extraction, while Felixstowe in Suffolk has the largest container port in the UK.

Going further north there is Nottingham, home of the household name of Boots the Chemist, and the brewing town of Burton-on-Trent, which was once completely criss-crossed by the private railways of the many brewing companies such as Bass Worthington, Truman's, Ind Coope and Charrington's, to name but a few.

Stour Valley line and Clare station

The small country town of Clare in Suffolk was served by the Stour Valley Railway (SVR), which was built and opened in stages from July 1849 to August 1865. It was a cross-country, single-track line with passing loops, and ran from the junction at Marks Tey station on the London to Colchester line of the Eastern Counties Railway (ECR). The SVR line then ran in a north-westerly direction to Haverhill, where it joined the Colne Valley & Halsted Railway to Shelford, a junction station on the main line of the London & North Western Railway (LNWR) to Cambridge.

The line served the small, prosperous, growing country towns of Sudbury, Long Melford, Clare, Haverhill and Bury St Edmunds. There were a total of 16 stations from Marks Tey to Cambridge, a total distance of 46.3 miles (74.5km). In the early days the line flourished with both passenger and goods traffic. The line ran along the picturesque Essex/Suffolk border, alongside the River Stour, which was made famous by the paintings of John Constable.

In 1862 the Eastern Counties Railway was amalgamated into the Great Eastern Railway (GER) group, and by 1923 into the London & North Eastern Railway (LNER) under the 'Grouping' brought about by the 1921 Railways Act. However, following nationalisation British Railways closed the branch from Melford to Bury St Edmunds in 1965, and from Shelford to Sudbury in 1967, which included Clare. The

The Great Eastern Railway's main station building at Clare, with ticket office, waiting room and toilet, opened in 1865 and was built to a standard GER design. There was a glazed canopy over the front entrance. The building has recently been reopend as a tea room

good news is that the line from Marks Tey to Sudbury is still open for business with hourly departures in each direction using diesel units. The first station after Marks Tey is Chappel & Wakes Colne, which is approached over the magnificent 1136-foot (346-metre) Chappel Viaduct of 32 arches that spans the River Colne valley at a height of 80 feet (24 metres).

The steam locomotives that regularly worked the line were:

GER 'Y14' (reclassified as LNER 'J15') 0-6-0s, built 1883-1913
GER 'S69' (reclassified as LNER 'B12') 4-6-0s, built 1911-28
GER 'T26' (reclassified as LNER 'E4') 2-4-0s, built 1892-1902

But more about Clare. The old station is within a stone's throw of the centre and is overlooked by the remains of Clare Castle, a medieval Norman castle keep on top of raised earthworks, both of which form part of the Clare Country Park with the River Stour winding its way through. Originally the castle had two baileys (enclosed courtyards) and defensive moats, but when the railway came to Clare the station was built on the site of the inner bailey. This must be a unique siting for a railway station.

The station building is still in good condition and is now in use as a tea room. There was a

The goods shed and crane both survive, with a token length of track going into the shed. The crane is undated but was manufactured by Richard Kitohin of Warrington.

Looking towards Sudbury, both platforms survive with a brick waiting room on the platform facing the main station building. The slope on the left side of the building is the remains of the cattle dock.

Below: This view is just past the station in the Sudbury direction looking across the bridge over Chilton Stream, which runs into the River Stour, then a straight stretch towards an overbridge and on to Cavendish and Long Melton.

This photo shows the rail bridge over the River Stour just after leaving Clare station in the Haverhill and Cambridge direction. The bridge was built in 1894 by Joseph Westwood of London.

passing loop through the station with an accommodating platform and waiting room. The two tracks have now been removed and the area grassed for public use. There was a signal box on the station building side, which has now been demolished.

Looking in the Sudbury direction, just past the end of the platform, the line crossed the River Stour over a two-road iron bridge that carried both the running line and loop line. Just beyond the river bridge the line passed under a small road bridge, then it was a reasonably straight run to Cavendish. Electric tablet working had been introduced between Sudbury and Clare in 1901 and a telegraph insulator is still mounted on the wall under the road bridge.

There was a small goods yard with a goods shed about 100 yards past the platform in the Cambridge direction. The yard is now open space laid to grass and the goods shed is being used for various activities. A short length of track protrudes from under the double doors of the shed, and the crane, made in Warrington by Kitohin, still resides on its brick plinth. In one corner of the small car park, just past the goods shed, a path leads down to where another rail bridge crosses the river at an angle; the bridge was built by Joseph Westwood & Co Ltd of London in 1894. Mounted on the side of the bridge are LNER brackets of 1933 vintage that held the pulleys for the signal cables.

Although no steam locomotives will puff their way along the Stour Valley again, it is worth a visit to this lovely and unique location in Suffolk to soak up the atmosphere of a bygone age.

Chappel & Wakes Colne station and East Anglian Railway Museum

As mentioned above, this station is the first stop from Marks Tey on this Greater Anglia line, known as 'the Gainsborough Line', to Sudbury.

Immediately before entering the station the line crosses the magnificent Chappel Viaduct over the River Colne and the Colchester Road. The viaduct, built between 1847 and 1849, contains seven million bricks made from local clay and is 1,066 feet (325 metres) in length

Hunslet 0-6-0ST *King George* is seen here shunting a mixed freight train past Chappel North signal box at the museum in 2009.

At Marks Tey station, a Greater Anglia train hauled by a Class 90 electric heads up towards London. The Sudbury line, which is not electrified, branches to the right with its own platform.

This view of Chappel Viaduct in perfect weather clearly shows the magnificent arches with a National Express One two-car DMU slowing to stop at Chappel & Wakes Colne station just the other side of the viaduct.

and consists of 32 arches, each having a 30-foot (9.14-metre) span and standing 75 feet (22.9 metres) above the valley floor.

Chappel & Wakes Colne station opened on 2 July 1849 at the same time as the Stour Valley Railway to Sudbury and is 3.6 miles (5.81km) from Marks Tey. It was built with three platforms but only Platform 1 is used by Greater Anglia Railways, as the line is now single track only. The station is now unmanned.

Platforms 2 and 3 are now used by the East Anglian Railway Museum, together with the existing sidings, goods shed and signal boxes. The main station building and signal boxes have been restored by the museum to post-war style and entry is via a ground-floor door. The museum was established in 1968, and became a registered charity in 1995. It has a display area and several steam locomotives, a couple in operational condition, and some diesel locomotives, together with two British Rail Class 101 DMUs built in 1958.

King George, built by Hunslet in Leeds in 1942, is an 0-6-0 saddle tank locomotive that originally served for many years in Nottingham collieries, enjoying retirement at the museum in 2009.

Left: This photo shows one of the two Class 101 DMUs, built in 1958, used for short trips within the museum.

Below: A photo taken from the museum platform in 2009 shows National Express One Class 153 'Super Sprinter' DMU No 153314; these were modified from two-car Class 155s to single units and entered service in 1991. This DMU is just arriving at Chappel station, and will then continue on to terminate at Marks Tey.

Manningtree and Harwich

Manningtree station and junction are on the Greater Anglia Liverpool Street-Ipswich-Norwich main line, which is electrified using a 25kVa 50Hz AC overhead catenary. Manningtree is situated at the limit of tidal flow of the River Stour, which forms the boundary between Essex and Suffolk.

Going north, the main line leaves Manningtree station and immediately crosses a bridge over the

Class 321 EMU No 321419, built in 1988 by BR Engineering, York, approaches Harwich International station (formerly Parkeston Quay) from the Manningtree direction. The terminus at Harwich Town is only a short distance further on; it is now just a single line and the station building is in a rather run-down area.

This photo was taken in the mid-1970s at Mistley Maltings on the Manningtree-Harwich branch just after the 'Brighton Belle' was withdrawn from service and bought by Allied Breweries, which then used the Pullman coaches as static restaurant cars within the grounds of its public houses. To the left a Class 08 diesel with a rake of steel container wagons has just ascended the 1 in 50 gradient from the quayside on the River Stour.

Crossing the bridge at Manningtree to enter the station just beyond is a local service formed by Class 360 EMU No 360102, consisting of four-car stock built in 2002 by Siemens.

Having just left the port of Felixstowe a train of loaded containers headed by Freightliner Class 66 No 66420 races across the bridge over the River Stour at Manningtree towards Colchester.

river into Suffolk heading towards Ipswich. At Ipswich a line heads towards Woodbridge and Halesworth where a branch at Westerfield runs down to Felixstowe to serve the large container port that is directly opposite Harwich on the Essex side.

Just a couple of hundred yards north of Manningtree station and before the bridge, a line branches east at the junction, running alongside the River Stour, through Mistley and down to the station at Harwich International Ferry Port, terminating at Harwich Town station.

The main-line is extremely busy with a constant flow of container trains, Greater Anglia expresses and local trains.

A Greater Anglia Liverpool Street to Norwich train crosses the Stour bridge having just left Manningtree station. The motive power provided by the Class 90 is at the rear of the train in 'push' mode, with a Class 82 Driving Van Trailer at the front.

Greater Anglia Class 90 No 90006 heads a Liverpool Street train as it runs over the level crossing just before arriving at Manningtree station. The Class 90s were built by BR Engineering at Crewe between 1987 and 1990 and are capable of 110mph (177km/h). The Harwich line can be seen branching to the right directly after the level crossing.

Halesworth station and crossing

Halesworth is a small country town in Suffolk on the East Suffolk line that runs from Ipswich to Lowestoft with interchanges for main-line connections. The station was built in 1859 and from 1879 became an interchange for the Southwold Railway, a 3-foot (914.4mm) narrow-gauge line to Southwold on the east coast, a distance of 8 miles (12.8km), which had its terminus adjacent to Halesworth station, but closed in 1929.

As time moved on and passengers became more confident about using the railway, passenger traffic increased considerably to merit longer trains, which meant increasing the length of platforms. In many cases this was a comparatively straightforward task, but at Halesworth the situation of the roads and properties surrounding the station only allowed extending at one end, but the Halesworth to Bungay road crossed the line immediately at the end of the original platform.

The solution was to build new movable crossing gates with wooden platforms on top at the same level as the original platform. These were built and installed in 1888 and increased the length of both up and down platforms.

The four new movable platforms weighed 7 tons each and were moved manually on small wheels at the end that ran over the wooden inlaid floor between the tracks. The platforms/gates were locked into position for safety from the signal box. There were also two small sections, one on each side of the tracks and opposite each other, that could be used by pedestrians or cyclists if the gates were closed to road traffic.

The gates were renewed by Boulton & Paul of Norwich in 1922, and this unique crossing remained in service until 1958 when the increase in road traffic demanded a new Halesworth-Bungay road to be constructed with a bridge built over the line. The crossing was then left to deteriorate and, with lack of any maintenance, became unusable.

However, all was not lost as the gates have been cosmetically restored and remain a fine example of British invention.

Above left: The cosmetically restored crossing still forms part of the platform for trains to Ipswich. The road behind, once the throughway over the railway, is now blocked off.

Left: The Boulton & Paul manufacturer's plate clearly shows that the platform was made in Norwich in 1922.

Above right: Ipswich-bound Abelio Greater Anglia Class 153 No 153322 passes the old crossing and glides smoothly into Halesworth station during October 2015. These 'Super Sprinters' came into service between 1991 and 1992. Originally built by Leyland Bus in 1997-98, they were converted to Class 153s by Hunslet-Barclay. Greater Anglia has five in service.

Left: This photograph dates back to the 1950s and graphically shows the platforms swinging open to allow traffic on the Halesworth-Bungay road to cross the line. The station building is to the left, on the Lowestoft side. The photo is dated by the dark green Post Office Telephones Morris van. *Halesworth Museum*

Left: GB Railfreight Class 66 No 66742, hauling 28 CovHop PA private-owner wagons of WBB Minerals, which were acquired by GBRf, is seen here in transit from Sibelco's sand quarry at Leziate in Norfolk to a Yorkshire glass works. *Adrian Booth*

Below: The standard-gauge sand loading plant at Middleton Towers station (known as Leziate) is the terminus of the 3-mile (4.8km) freight-only line from King's Lynn. The wagons are under the control of two four-wheel mechanical shunters built by F. C. Hibberd of Park Royal, London, circa 1990. *Simon Mace, Sibelco*

Norfolk sand

Apart from the substance we associate with holidays and beaches, there is also high-quality silica sand that has many industrial uses, in particular the production of sheet glass and bottles and auto glass, and is normally extracted from carefully chosen surface pits.

One major area for silica sand extraction is Middleton Towers, some 4 miles (6.4km) from King's Lynn in Norfolk, which has been in operation since the mid-19th century. Transporting the sand away was obviously a major issue and the local railway companies played their part by providing sidings where it could be loaded.

The areas of extraction are sandwiched between the lines of two former railway companies. One was the Lynn & Dereham Railway (L&DR), which opened in October 1846 with the first station from King's Lynn being Middleton, where sidings were provided for the developing sand pits; the line then continued to Swaffham, Dereham and Norwich.

The other railway company was the Midland & Great Northern Joint Railway (M&GNJR), which operated from its terminus at South Lynn station with sidings provided for loading sand at Gayton Road. This single-track line continued in a north-easterly direction to Fakenham, Thursford, Holt, Weybourne, Sheringham and Cromer. The M&GNJR was formed in 1893 to give access to the north Norfolk coast and benefitted from the increasing numbers of holidaymakers from the Midlands and the North of England. The single track between Dereham and Middleton, later a part of British Rail Eastern Region, was closed under the Beeching 'Axe' in 1968, but the sand company was provided with a run-round loop siding and an overhead sand-loading gantry at Middleton.

As the sand pit expanded a 1ft 11½in (598mm) narrow-gauge railway system was constructed within it, which by the early 1990s stretched between the two standard-gauge sidings, about 1 mile apart, incorporating a large circular track and many sidings off to the working faces. Hudson-type steel side-tipping wagons were used, hauled by a succession of four-wheeled diesel and petrol-motored engines built by John Fowler (two), F. C. Hibberd (three), Motor Rail (three) and Doncaster (one). Dates of construction ranged from 1919 to 1964.

The narrow-gauge railway was closed in June 1977 and replaced

Above: During the quarry's former ownership by British Industrial Sand Ltd, this 0-6-0ST, named *Peter* and built by Hudswell Clarke of Leeds in 1929, Works No 1640, worked at the Gayton Road station sidings until 1968. *Frank Jones*

Below left GB Railfreight Class 66 No 66737 is hauling its empty wagons to the modern overhead sand-loading plant at Leziate. The track to the right is the run-round loop. Further down the line is the closed Middleton Towers station and adjacent level crossing. *Simon Mace, Sibelco*

Below: At the modern high-speed sand-loading plant at the Sibelco location, known as Leziate, GBRf No 66737 has its rake of bogie wagons loaded with sand for onward delivery to a Yorkshire glass works. *Simon Mace, Sibelco*

A standard-gauge four-wheeled diesel locomotive built in the 1950s by F. C. Hibberd pulls a 24.5-tonne steel hopper wagon of type HJV under the old sand loading plant at Leziate. *Simon Mace, Sibelco*

The 2-foot (610mm) narrow-gauge system into the working quarry areas utilised four-wheeled diesel-mechanical locomotives built by Motor Rail Ltd of Bedford. This one is Works No 11297, built in 1955, seen here hauling Hudson steel side-tipping wagons under a minor road. Note the low headroom. *Simon Mace, Sibelco*

by a conveyor belt system from the pit areas to the stock piles and loading-out gantry. The standard-gauge siding at Gayton Road was removed by April 1966.

The current owner of the silica sand pits is Sibelco UK Ltd, and production today from Middleton Towers, which is now named Leziate, amounts to 130,000 tonnes per annum. Most of the prepared sand is sent out by rail each weekday, primarily to the Yorkshire companies of Guardian Glass at Goole and Ardagh Glass at both Doncaster and Barnsley for the production of high-quality glass. Daily weekday trains arrive at Leziate at 5.00am and depart at 7.30am, with the second train arriving at 10.20am and departing at 12.30pm to 2.00pm. These trains are hauled by GB Railfreight Class 66s with around 25 four-wheeled covered hopper wagons.

In the late 1960s the sand pits were owned by British Industrial Sand, which owned a fleet of covered hopper wagons advertising its prime customers such as the Rockware Glass brand, now owned by Ardagh Glass Ltd of Doncaster, which acquired this former Greenford, London, company in 2006. Other hopper wagons were signed with 'WBB Minerals', painted white with a broad sand-coloured band.

This aerial view of the Leziate sand works shows the standard-gauge tracks running left to right. King's Lynn is 3 miles (4.8km) to the left. The narrow-gauge feeder system heads north to the extensive sand quarries. *Simon Mace, Sibelco Laziate sand quarry, Norfolk*

Captain William Peel's Sandy & Potton Railway

Captain William Peel VC KCB was the third son of Prime Minister Sir Robert Peel. He served in the Royal Navy with distinction, being awarded the Victoria Cross for gallantry for three conspicuous actions in the Dardanelles. He commanded several ships, including HMS *Shannon*, an early sail and steam frigate, and while sailing to China was diverted to India where he contracted smallpox, having been wounded by a musket ball. He died on 27 April 1858 at the age of only 33.

William Peel owned a large estate of 1,400 acres (5.7km²) between Sandy and Potton in Bedfordshire. The Great Northern Railway opened its main line in 1850 with a double-track station at Sandy, and this spurred William Peel to consider a railway line connecting to his estate to assist in the development of his agricultural business. He owned large portions of land except near Sandy, so he began purchasing the intervening land to the west of his estate, which then permitted him to construct a single-track standard-gauge branch line. As he owned all the necessary land he was not required to have an Act of Parliament for its construction. Work commenced in May 1856 on the private railway 3 miles 2 furlongs (4.8km) long. The line

CAPTAIN PEEL'S RAILWAY.

A PUBLIC MEETING

WILL BE HELD AT THE

CROWN INN, POTTON,

ON

Tuesday May 26th, 1857,

At TEN o'Clock in the Forenoon.

TO DECIDE UPON STEPS TO BE TAKEN ON THE

DAY OF OPENING

This Railway. All persons interested, are requested to attend.

Potton, May, 25th, 1857.

TEBBUTT, PRINTER, POTTON.

A public notice proclaiming the opening of Captain Peel's Railway on Tuesday 26 May 1857.

branched off from Sandy station, then ran in a southerly direction for a short distance parallel with the main line. It then curved through 90 degrees eastward towards Potton and up a gradient of 1 in 100.

Left: Sandy station on the former LNWR line, originally part of the private S&PR, which struck off in an easterly direction to Potton. *Marcus Johnson*

Below: This delightful 0-4-0 tank engine used in the construction of the line was named *Shannon* after the Captain's naval ship. Built by George England & Co in 1857, it was subsequently sold to the Wantage Tramway in 1878, then purchased by the GWR in 1945 for preservation.

The line was ceremoniously opened for business on 25 June 1857, with Peel's wife carrying out the formalities as he was abroad on duty. The cost of the construction was £15,000, paid for by Captain Peel. For the construction of the branch line the Captain purchased an 0-4-0 well tank locomotive, named *Shannon* after HMS *Shannon*, which cost £800 and was built by George England & Co Ltd of Hatcham, New Cross, south London.

The station at Potton was very basic, handling outward traffic of fruit and vegetables, with soot and horse manure inwards for fertiliser from London via Sandy station. At Potton there was a goods shed and brick-built engine shed with a small office; both structures have now been demolished. Rolling stock for the line, besides two passenger coaches, would have consisted of a few covered vans for the perishable fruits and packages, with several open wagons for the manure and coal, etc. Bradshaw quotes that there were two passenger trains consisting of two coaches in the morning and two in the afternoon in each direction. Tickets were 9d for 1st Class, 6d for 2nd Class and 3d for 3rd Class. The journey time between Sandy and Potton was just 10 minutes!

In 1862 the Bedford & Cambridge Railway acquired Captain Peel's railway, doubling the track and extending the line eastwards to Cambridge, in order to complete its east-to-west cross-country railway between the university cities of Oxford and Cambridge via Bicester, Claydon, Verney Junction, Bedford and Sandy.

This line became known as the 'Varsity Line', and fell victim to Dr Beeching's closure programme on 1 January 1968.

Shannon was sent to Crewe for shunting duties, and was then sold in 1878 to the Wantage Tramway; on the closure of the tramway the Great Western Railway purchased the diminutive loco for £100, restored it and placed it on display under a canopy on Wantage station. Today it is in a fine steaming condition at the Didcot Railway Centre.

With the doubling of the track by the LNWR a new substantial station was built at Potton with decorative contrasting brickwork and a coal yard, cattle dock and two sidings to receive soot from Liverpool, Manchester and Sheffield, besides London.

Today the platforms and the station building remain in private ownership, complete with the

Left The cast-iron spandrels of Potton's platform canopy are dated 1862 and includes the initials 'BC' for the Bedford & Cambridge Railway, which was later absorbed by the LNWR.

Below left This semaphore distant signal stands at the former 'Locomotive' public house in Potton, which commemorates the line's steam engine.

Below Much of Potton station still exists in private ownership, including the platforms, canopy, gradient signs and station buildings.

cast-iron columns and spandrels incorporating 'BC' for the Bedford & Cambridge Railway; this also short-lived railway company was absorbed by the LNWR in July 1865.

Close by Potton station were two public houses, 'The King's Hussars' and 'The Locomotive'. The latter was originally a beer house licensed in 1836 and was owned by Potton brewer Francis Bingham. It became a free house and was then acquired by local brewer Charles Wells in 1903. The pub closed early in the 21st century but an upper-quadrant signal on the front forecourt still stands to this day, commemorating the former cross-country 'Varsity Line'.

The Sandy & Potton Railway, or Captain Peel's Railway, was the shortest in length and shortest in life of any standard-gauge public railway, and is now just a pleasant memory.

However, the 'Varsity Line' is now considered to be important to our future and, although partially derelict in places, is considered to be reopenable. We wait and see!

'Boots, for Health and Beauty'

No matter what age you are there has always been a 'Boots the Chemist' or, as it is today, just 'Boots', in your local High Street. It has managed to survive the ups and downs of combining both its manufacturing and retail interests since the mid-1800s to become one of the most respected and renowned organisations in the UK.

The founding of this massive organisation began in the 19th century when Jesse Boot set up his first shop in Nottingham. With business rapidly expanding, more shops were opened,

A view of one of the platforms showing one of the loading and unloading areas of the Boots plant. All had a canopy to reduce the effects of the elements. *Judith Wright, Boots*

forming the basis of the huge Boots empire of today, which requires a highly professional organisation manufacturing a vast range of products involving ordering of raw materials, warehousing, packaging and despatch.

As the company expanded it acquired a green-field site at Beeston, a south-west suburb of Nottingham, bounded to the west by the former London Midland & Scottish Railway (LMS) main line and to the east by the Beeston Canal. The site was opened in 1929 with a soap works and its own power station. The entire layout of the modernist buildings and services ensured that goods moved easily through each stage of production in a continuous flow. The continued growth of Boots' 'clean and healthy' products reflected the 1920s and '30s 'Health and Beauty' movement across Europe, where cleanliness and outdoor pursuits were uppermost in the developing world. Further expansion saw more modernist-style buildings on the 340-acre site being built from 1933. These beautifully stylish buildings were designed by Sir Owen Williams and the site was claimed to be the largest pharmaceutical factory in the world, coming on stream in 1936. Two of these buildings have since been

An aerial view of the Boots complex, clearly showing the internal rail connections into the various manufacturing areas. All the connections came together into a transfer siding for goods inward and outward travel via the LMS main line. *Judith Wright, Boots*

Left: The unmistakable household name of Boots, with a logo that we see in virtually every high street in the UK.

Below: This interesting view inside one of the manufacturing areas clearly shows the beautifully designed modernist architecture compatible with pharmaceutical manufacturing. Seen also is the smokeless locomotive absolutely necessary in that environment. *Judith Wright, Boots*

Grade I listed, with the remaining buildings Grade II listed.

Boots had constructed its own internal standard-gauge railway to serve each building. Raw materials arriving and manufactured products leaving the plant did so by rail. A curved siding left the LMS main line, ran into Boots' premises and divided into a loop permitting the LMS shunting locomotive to run round the wagons brought in from the freight yard opposite. Loaded vans and empty tank wagons would be taken out the same way. Movement of wagons in and out of the various buildings was then the responsibility of Boots' own locomotive, as cleanliness was paramount.

Each building was designed to incorporate its own railway sidings, with a total of 10 sidings connected to a head shunt running parallel to the canal. Several buildings had two sidings running inside their full length with loading

A view showing staff unloading raw materials from an open wagon. *Judith Wright, Boots*

This is *Puffing Billy*, the smokeless 0-4-0 locomotive built in 1935 by Andrew Barclay of Kilmarnock, Scotland. The staff look clearly proud of their locomotive. *Judith Wright, Boots*

and unloading capabilities on each side of the building's interior, and overhead canopies where the loading and unloading areas were open to the elements.

Each building's ground floor was raised to the height of a railway wagon floor for ease of handling. Elevators took raw materials to the appropriate departments, including cellars, where a range of storage tanks held olive oil. Throughout the warehousing and despatch buildings, a conveyor system connected the various sites with the assembly areas for orders to be despatched by rail. As each year passed new products were introduced, and as early as the 1930s beauty was the outward sign of good health, so toilet preparations and similar cosmetic preparations became an integral part of Boots' chemist shops.

As cleanliness was a real issue, the locomotive chosen to move materials in and out of the buildings was an Andrew Barclay 0-4-0 fireless locomotive, No 2008 built in 1935 and named *Puffing Billy*. This fireless loco obtained its steam from the Boots power house, which provided steam power to the entire factory and offices. In 1955 the unusual 'steamer' was replaced by another 'clean' loco, this time a Ruston Hornsby 0-4-0 diesel, No 384139, built in Lincoln, which continued the good work of transportation in the works. Boots' private railway finally came to an end in May 1981, giving way to road transport.

The shopping list of raw materials used at Beeston is almost endless. For the initial soap factory, caustic soda came in 10-ton railway tank wagons. Fats and oils were delivered in large barrels containing coconut oil, palm oil, cod liver oil from Norway, and local animal fats. Also imported were herbs, minerals, quinine from Peru, peppermint, eucalyptus from Australia, camphor from Japan and honey from the West Indies – just a very few of the ingredients brought to Beeston, many of which came from around the world.

As with many developing businesses, amalgamations and take-overs are commonplace. Boots today is the first global pharmacy-led Health and Wellbeing enterprise, trading in 25 countries and employing 385,000 people, with 390 distribution centres delivering to 230,000 pharmacies, doctors, health centres, hospitals and retail outlets. Boots acquired a long-standing competitor, Timothy Whites & Taylors, in 1968. In 2012 Walgreens bought a 45% stake in Alliance Boots with a three-year option to buy the remainder, which was taken up in 2014.

Great Central Railway

The Great Central Railway (GCR) had the distinction of being the last main line in the United Kingdom. Formed in 1847 as the Manchester, Sheffield & Lincolnshire Railway, it changed its name in 1897 to the Great Central Railway in anticipation of its extension going south to London, which opened in 1899.

The north was the industrial powerhouse of England, and GCR lines formed a complex network from Liverpool on the west coast via Manchester, Sheffield, Bradford and Leeds to Grimsby, Immingham and Hull on the east coast, to name but a few. The new 92-

A rural view of the GCR heritage railway in 2009 features BR Standard Class 2MT 2-6-0 No 78019 with its four passenger coaches heading towards Leicester. The loco was designed by Riddles and was built at Darlington Works in 1954, withdrawn in 1966 and arrived at the GCR in 1998. It was then overhauled and returned to steam in 2004.

A perfect spring day, and ex-LNER Class 'N2' 0-6-2T No 69621 makes its way over the road bridge by Swithland Sidings. On the far side is the junction of the Mountsorrel Railway, leading to the quarry of the same name.

mile (147km) London Extension offered an alternative high-speed, main-line service via Nottingham, Leicester, Loughborough and Rugby down the centre of England to London. The GCR network then looked like a giant 'T' when viewed on a rail map.

The London Extension was constructed from Annesley in Nottinghamshire to join the Metropolitan Railway outpost at Quainton Road in Buckinghamshire, which was 44 miles (71km) from London, then had its own tracks from Canfield Place near Finchley Road for the final run into Marylebone station on the north-west side of London.

The GCR had several noteworthy leaders, including Edward Watkin, who, apart from being Chairman of the GCR, was conveniently Chairman of the Metropolitan Railway, which no doubt was a positive factor in the building of the extension.

In the years that followed the GCR formed alliances and joint committees with other railway companies to increase its outreach, such as the London & North Western Railway (LNWR), and the Great Northern Railway (GNR), which initially gave it access into King's Cross. The GCR was rapidly gaining a

reputation for fast services to and from London, and in 1902 introduced an express service from Bournemouth and Southampton to York and Newcastle-upon-Tyne. In 1903 it ran a non-stop service from London to Sheffield, a distance of 163.75 miles (262km) in 3 hours at an average speed of 55.6mph (89km/h). Passengers who desired to disembark at Leicester or Nottingham occupied slip coaches at the back of the train that were released at the appropriate time.

Locomotives for the GCR were built at the company's Gorton Works in Manchester and by several outside manufacturers such as Beyer Peacock, Kitson, Neilson, Fairbairn and Sharp Stewart. The heavy coal traffic required powerful locomotives designed by several engineers. Classes included the 'A' 0-6-2T, the '8' 4-6-0 for the Grimsby fish traffic, and the '8A' 0-8-0, some redesigned as The Class 'Q1' f0-8-0T. There were also the Class '8H' 0-8-4Ts and Robinson's Class '8K' 2-8-0s, of which 521 were built during the First World War.

Along the east coast the docks continued to develop, with the GCR moving vast quantities of coal from its heartland for export using some of its own ships. It also ran special coal trains

A mixed freight train near Rothley in 2012 has BR Riddles Class 4MT 2-6-4T No 80072 at the business end. This loco was built at Brighton Works in 1953 and withdrawn in 1965. It was retrieved from Barry scrapyard in 1988 and rebuilt to the splendid condition seen here.

A view of Quorn & Woodhouse station from the station yard shows the island platform between the main up and down lines that was typical of GCR London Extension stations. The train arriving is headed by Ivatt/LMS Class 2 2-6-0 No 46521, built in 1953 at Swindon Works and withdrawn in 1966; it arrived at the GCR in 2001 and was in steam in 2011.

A good example of GCR station design with the island platform and central footbridge coming down from the road is provided by Rothley station in 2009.

from South Wales to Immingham Docks to assist in the war effort up to 1919, and a similar arrangement to Scotland for the Royal Navy fleet at Scapa Flow.

The grand and youngest main line railway company was finally dissolved on 1 January 1923 when it became part of the London &

North Eastern Railway. Sadly, as a result of the Beeching 'Axe' it was closed as a through route in 1966, although a section between Nottingham and Rugby remained open until 1969.

An old postcard of GCR locomotive *Sir Sam Fay*, John Robinson-designed Class 'B2' 4-6-0 No 423 built at the GCR's Gorton Works in 1912. Sir Sam Fay was the General Manager of the GCR, rising to that position after joining the railway in 1872 as a clerk. He died in 1953 aged 91. Unfortunately, these locos did not perform to expectations and were withdrawn in 1947. None have survived into preservation.

The cover of the GCR's 1903 timetables features a flamboyant layout and the GCR crest, and not only advertises rail services but also the company's cross-Channel steamer fleet to Rotterdam, Hamburg and Antwerp. No roll, roll off in those days!

The Great Central Railway in preservation

By the time of the final line closure, enthusiasts had formed the Main Line Preservation Group (MLPG) and in 1970 managed to lease Loughborough station, buildings and trackbed, while also continuing to salvage as much of the original materials from demolition. By 1973 short public rides were available using small industrial locomotives.

In 1976 it became Great Central Railway Plc, which allowed the company to raise money by selling shares for purchasing more track. Initially, only single track could be relaid between Loughborough and Quorn & Woodhouse, with Rothley coming later. By the late 1980s the line was further extended to Belgrave & Birstall, but the station had to be demolished and a new station, Leicester North, was built a short distance south, inside Leicester's city boundary. Since the 1990s the single track has been doubled to allow more trains to run, with new signal boxes and Great Western-style signals. It is now the only standard-gauge railway in preservation that has double track outside station areas.

Currently the line runs for 8.25 miles (13.2km) from Leicester North to Loughborough, but work is progressing to connect with the separately preserved Loughborough-Nottingham section, which will increase the line to 18 miles (28.8km). However, major obstacles need to be overcome; a new bridge over the Midland main line just outside Loughborough has been installed, but a canal bridge needs refurbishment. These two bridges will be joined by new embankments and concrete arches and the line will initially be single track.

Mountsorrel Railway

This was a standard-gauge 8½-mile (13.6km) network of industrial railway lines that served the Mountsorrel Granite Company from around 1860, and was connected to the GCR at Swithland Sidings. It then ran around the quarries to the Midland main line at Barrow-upon-Soar. The railway was closed in the 1950s and the quarries are now owned by Lafarge Aggregates. Over the last few years volunteers have relaid 1.25 miles (2km) of track from Swithland Sidings, and this line was opened to the public in October 2015. The work continues!

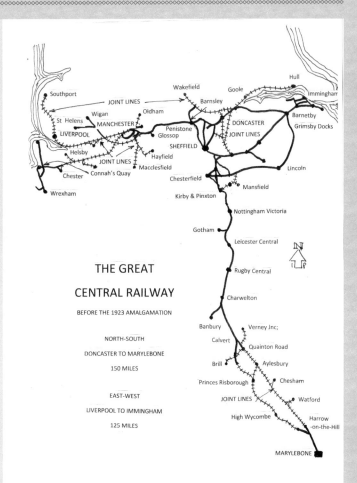

THE GREAT

CENTRAL RAILWAY

BEFORE THE 1923 AMALGAMATION

NORTH-SOUTH

DONCASTER TO MARYLEBONE

150 MILES

EAST-WEST

LIVERPOOL TO IMMINGHAM

125 MILES

This big feller is John Robinson-designed Class '8H' 0-8-4T No 1173, built by Beyer Peacock in 1908 for the purpose of 'hump shunting'. A freight yard would have a purpose-built hump up which wagons would be pushed and allowed to free-wheel to their designated sidings to make up freight trains. At the time of building these locomotives were the most powerful in the UK.

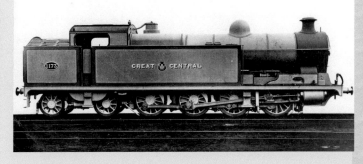

ENGLAND'S LATEST PORT

IMMINGHAM *Grimsby* COALING JETTY

'England's Latest Port': Immingham, the GCR's deep-water coaling jetty, as depicted in a period advertisement when coal was supreme and Britain's major export.

One of the most prolific locomotive designs in Britain: a Great Central '8K' 2-8-0 designed by Robinson, 521 of which were built during the First World War period.

Bass & Co 0-4-0ST locomotive No 3, built in 1891 (Works No 609) by the local company of Thornewill & Warham, approaches Church Croft Junction signal box in May 1960. *H. C. Casserley*

Burton-on-Trent brewery railways

There is no other town in Britain that has had such a wealth of railways in such a confined area as Burton-on-Trent. This was due to a history of brewing that dates back to 1295, when beer was brewed at the Abbey because the water was found to be most suitable. Over the years the brewing industry grew and by 1839 the Midland Railway (MR) had come to Burton from Birmingham, and immediately the few premier brewers who had been established since the early 1700s rapidly took advantage of the railways for bringing in barley and malt, and coal for raising steam, but mostly for exporting to a wider customer base both at home and abroad. The two prime brewers in those early days were Bass and Allsopps, and others soon followed from London. Ind Coope of Romford, Truman and Charrington soon built their new breweries

to produce India Pale Ale; this was recognised as the most popular beer, as it travelled well to the far places of the Empire, especially for the British tea-growers and the military during the Victorian era.

The premier and earliest breweries were located near the Midland Railway, but as the town expanded many smaller breweries built further outward. Each required maltings, cooperages and bottling facilities, and to transport the raw materials between the different departments to the brew houses private railway systems were built. The MR was soon followed into Burton by the London & North Western Railway (LNWR) and shortly afterwards by the North Staffordshire Railway, all wanting to cash in on the lucrative business. The MR built its engine sheds opposite the Leicester Junction to the west of the town, while the LNWR was on the Derby side of town. The Wetmore Sidings and Dixie Sidings on both sides of the main line dealt with the assembly of hundreds of wagons

This photo, taken in 1933, shows Bass locomotive No 11, an 0-4-0ST built by Neilson Reid in 1899, pulling a mixed rake of open and covered wagons from the sidings. *H. C. Casserley*

Bass fleet loco 0-4-0 No 2 is seen at one of the many crossing in Burton. *R. C. Riley*

and the despatch of brewery traffic. The MR was the dominant railway company, and built branch lines around the town such as the Bond End and Guild Street branches, from which numerous private sidings served the many breweries and their associated departments. One of the major products of brewing is a surplus of yeast, and near the Leicester Junction were factory sidings built for household names such as Branston and Marmite. These branch lines and the private sidings had to cross public roads in the town by some 24 level crossings, complete with gates

and signal boxes controlling semaphore signals, all operated in a very professional manner.

Allsopps was the first brewery to take delivery of a steam engine in 1862, followed a year later by Bass, with an 0-4-0 tank engine built locally by Burton's own engine builder, Thornewill & Warham, now still in business as Briggs.

Bass – or Bass, Ratcliff & Gretton, to give its full title – had some 20 miles of private sidings that were shunted by approximately a dozen engines that were 'on duty' at any one time.

Bass also had a private coach for taking visitors around the system.

In total Bass operated 28 locomotives in Midland Railway red livery. Allsopps had nine locomotives in dark green livery, Ind Coope had 11 in Brunswick Green, Worthington had 16 and Marston with five in dark blue. Also Salts Breweries had four locomotives painted in a brownish maroon colour, and Truman, Hanbury & Buxton had five in a mid-green livery.

Apart from these colourful locomotives, several of the brewery companies in Burton, including Bass, Worthington, Ind Coope, Allsopps and Truman, had their own private-owner wagons with company liveries displayed along the sides. Allsopps and Truman both used bulk tanker wagons for despatch to regional brewers for bottling, especially Allsopps with its early lager beer, while Bass and

Worthington often despatched their products in elaborately signed covered vans. A number of brewery-owned wooden wagons for internal use were commonplace around Burton.

As well as the important beer products being transported out of the breweries, a number of ingredients were required to be transported inwards for the breweries to function. Vast quantities of coal and coke were brought in by collieries' own rolling stock, which was required at each location around the town for steam boilers; these were usually located where there were water wells, which were most necessary for maltings, where the barley had to be constantly wetted. Also, large amounts of the vital barley and malt, mainly from maltings in East Anglia, were constantly shipped in to the breweries.

However, by the 1960s the brewing industry in Burton was in decline. There are probably a number of reasons, such as amalgamations and takeovers, and a need for more spacious and modern brewing facilities to compete in more international markets. Also, Beeching's plan for the modern railway network probably had some influence, as he was determined to eliminate small mixed freight services in favour of more block train movements, especially for coal. Last but not least, the advent of motorways allowed for faster door-to-door transportation of both goods in and out.

Today there is virtually nothing left, but we should not forget that the four major brewers between them had 40 miles of private railway tracks, which in their heyday despatched from Burton each year 400,000 wagons. Burton is a town of beer and for many years stood apart from all other towns as a railway metropolis without any rivals.

R. C. Riley

Morning 'steam-up' outside the two Bass locomotive sheds in 1961. The locomotive on the right is being coaled up, while a locomotive with a rake of wagons weaves its way through the yard. *R. C. Riley*

The Bass sheds are in the left background as another 0-4-0 locomotive hauls a rake of coal wagons over another of the many road crossings in the town. *R. C. Riley*

A former S. Allsopp & Sons two-road engine shed accommodates locos in Ind Coope and Allsopp livery, circa 1958. On the left are Baguley diesels Nos 1 and 2 (Works Nos 3227 and 3357) built in 1951 and 1952, while on the right are an English Electric four-wheel 240V battery locomotive (Works No 533) built in 1922 and a Sentinel four-wheel loco (Works No 9376), built in 1947. *R. C. Riley*

Below: Bass malt vans are being unloaded while a Neilson Reid 0-4-0ST shunts a Worthington rail tanker. Sharp curves set in cobblestones among high buildings were typical within large breweries. *R. C. Riley*

Above left: Ind Coope's first locomotive is seen at its Burton brewery in 1894. It is thought to have been built locally by Thornewill & Warham around 1863. It was a well tank with ornamental fluted dome, Salter safety valves, tall copper-flared chimney and no weather-proofing for the crew.

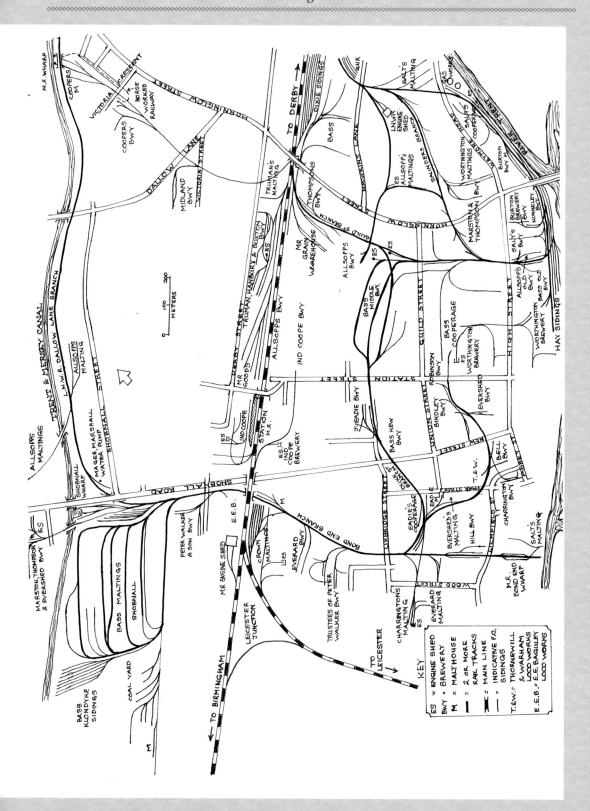

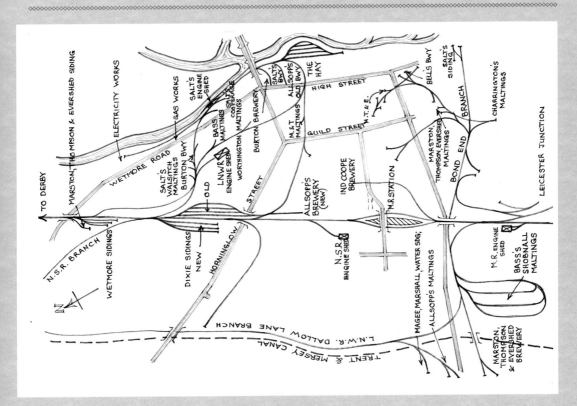

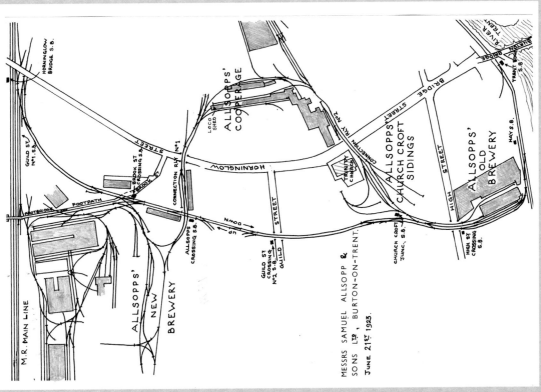

MESSRS SAMUEL ALLSOPP & SONS LTD, BURTON-ON-TRENT.
JUNE 21ST 1925.

Barrington Cement Works

Six miles south-west of Cambridge and midway between the old Roman road, Ermine Street, and its modern counterpart, the M11, lies the small Foxton station on the Cambridge-King's Cross main line, which branches from Shelford Junction on the West Anglia main line across to Hitchin Junction on the East Coast Main Line.

Foxton was the junction for the Barrington Light Railway, the shortest light railway in the UK, being only 1½ miles (2.4km) in length and opened in January 1926. It was built to service the Eastwood Cement Company, which was the first working owner of the chalk quarry cut into the low range of hills north of the village of Barrington. Leaving Foxton station the private line branched off, passing the transfer sidings and heading towards the quarry.

The line was built by contractor T. W. Ward Ltd of Sheffield to the standard gauge with the steepest gradient of 1 in 115; there was only one major construction, a ferro-concrete bridge of 235 yards (215 metres) spanning the infant River Cam. Being a light railway the locomotives were not to exceed 12 tons and the maximum speed was 25mph (40km/h). Although the railway did

Above: This view is looking north towards the quarrying hill and shows some loaded 'Internal User Only' wagons awaiting entry into the wagon tippler, manufactured by Strauchan & Henshaw of Bristol.

Right: 1963-built Ruston Hornsby 0-4-0 No 8 propels 16-ton wagons towards the tippler.

Right: At the reception sidings near the main line, a BR Class 47 waits to take out loaded 'Presflo' and tank wagons hauled by back-to-back Sentinels Nos 17 and 18.

Below right The two diesel-hydraulic Sentinels, Nos 17 and 18, built in 1960, are seen again at the reception sidings in front of some Rugby Cement tank wagons.

not carry paying passengers, workers could board the train at Foxton for the short journey to the quarry. At about the time of opening, a 2-foot (610mm) narrow-gauge tramway was also introduced to serve the working areas of the quarry.

The first steam locomotive at the cement works was a Barclay 0-4-0ST named *Vulcan*, built in 1909 and arriving on site in 1927. It was joined in 1933 by another similar Barclay, *Clydebank*, built in 1902, which was fitted with large wooden dumb buffers and remained until 1961. Thereafter there was a succession of four-wheeled diesel locos, built by Thomas Hill, Rolls-Royce, Sentinel and Ruston Hornsby.

Apart from quarrying chalk, several other raw materials were needed to manufacture cement, which required inward traffic of around 300-350 tons per week of crushed gypsum and around 2,000 tons per week of fine slack coal imported from Columbia via Immingham Docks for firing the several kilns. This volume of raw materials demanded a minimum of three trains a day, with additional trains arriving with empty cement and coal 'merry-go-round' wagons. Typical cement wagons included 'Presflo' 20-ton bulk wagons, 51-ton 'Procor' wagons and 12-ton 'Shocvans' for bagged cement.

During 1962 the Eastwood Cement Co became a part of the Rugby Portland Cement Co Ltd, and a modernisation programme was implemented with major changes in production methods, as production had increased to 6,000 tons of cement per week. The 2-foot (610mm) system in the quarry working areas was replaced by standard-gauge 75lb (35kg) bullhead rails, leaving the rolling stock surplus to requirements. The narrow-gauge system had utilised Hudson steel side-tipping 'V' wagons

hauled by an Orenstein & Koppel four-wheeled diesel-mechanical loco and a four-wheel DM Rolls-Royce built in 1959.

With the introduction of the standard gauge into the working areas of the quarry, a new wagon side-tipper device was installed by Strauchan & Henshaw of Bristol in 1963/64 and was the last of this type of machine to be in use in Britain. The loaded wagon would be clamped into the tippler, which would then tip them to an angle so the contents would be disgorged.

At the working faces of the quarry, both chalk and clay were excavated by Ruston Bucyrus face shovels with a boom of 80 feet (24.4 metres). Within the quarry there were some 50 'Internal User Only' steel wagons painted a pale aqua green. These wagons were propelled to the tippler by three standard-gauge 0-4-0 diesel locomotives, fleet Nos 7, 8 (Ruston Hornsby) and 15 (Thomas Hill), all built in 1963 and supplied new for the changeover of gauges.

Just before the light railway's connection with the main line at Foxton there were

Above: Four-wheel diesel-hydraulic locomotive No 15, built by Thomas Hill in 1963, propels 'Presflo' wagons under the loading plant.

Above right: A chalk-laden 16-ton steel wagon is being unloaded by the tipper. The quarry and storage sidings are to the right of the picture.

Right: A 16-ton steel internal user wagon being loaded. The loco is No 15, a 178hp diesel built by Thomas Hill and sporting green livery.

Below right: The back-to-back Sentinels of 1960 vintage, Nos 17 and 18, are hauling empty 'merry-go-round' hoppers over the River Cam.

three loop transfer sidings, which permitted BR Class 47 locomotives to bring in the coal and empty wagon trains, usually three times a day. The Rugby Cement company's locomotives brought down the empty wagons from the works and journeyed back and forth with usually three train loads of 700 tons for each delivery, requiring two Sentinel locos working in tandem. At the connection of the private railway with BR, there was only a light beam that informed the Foxton signalman of any activity; the connection was via a single loop line. Outward traffic of cement ceased in 1990 and the entire rail system was closed down in 2005.

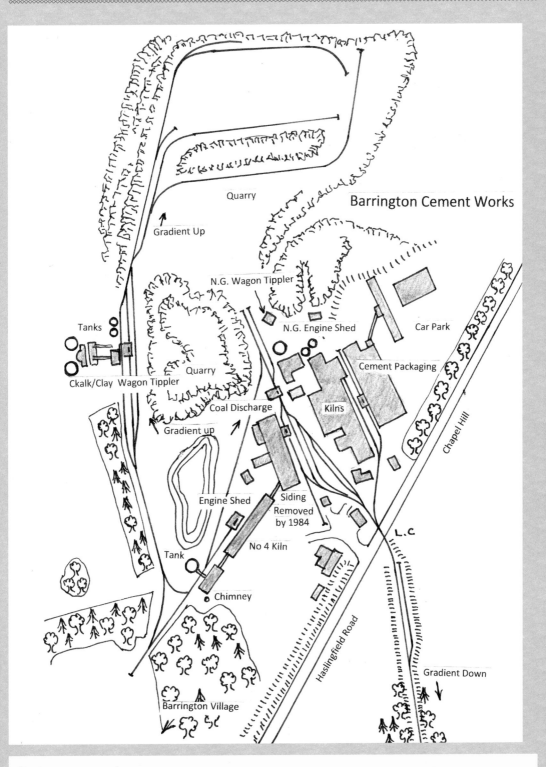

Barrington cement works

5. The North and Scotland

The North of England was the powerhouse of the Industrial Revolution, with locomotives like Stephenson's *Rocket* running on the Liverpool & Manchester Railway way back in 1829. The majority of England's railway history arises from the need to supply industry with raw materials and coal to the factories and transport manufactured goods around the UK and to ports for shipment to far-off lands – as we still had an Empire at that time! The industrial landscape has changed completely since then, but the history remains!

This section includes industrial glass-making in Yorkshire, and Carlisle station and the railway lines that feed it.

Scotland has two main rail links to England, from Glasgow Central down the West Coast Main Line and from Edinburgh Waverley down the East Coast Main Line. Glasgow also has another terminus at Queen Street. Between them these main stations serve all routes in Scotland with trains currently operated for ScotRail by the Abellio franchise.

In its time Scotland has produced some beautiful locomotives from builders like the North British company in Glasgow and the renowned industrial locomotive builder Andrew Barclay & Sons of Kilmarnock. Scottish railway companies such as the Caledonian Railway, the Glasgow & South Western Railway, the Highland Railway and the North British Railway all turned out beautifully coach-painted locomotives.

Scotland is never mentioned without the thought of the whisky industry, which relied heavily on the railways to transport its 'liquid gold', or a trip on the West Highland Line to take in the awe-inspiring splendour of the glens and mountains. But apart from these feel-good factors, back to the First World War the countryside along the Solway Firth near Gretna was turned into a giant munitions factory manufacturing vast quantities of highly volatile cordite for shells being used in France; Gretna was also, at that time, the scene of the worst railway disaster this country has known.

Wirksworth: the reluctant branch line

Wirksworth is a small and attractive market town at the head of the Ecclesbourne Valley in the Derbyshire High Peak district, and in the 1860s did not expect to have a railway line to Derby and beyond.

After the crazy days of the 'railway mania' in the 1840s the prominent railway companies that emerged were forced to make agreements, no matter how unpalatable, between each other to jointly use sections of lines to reach important destinations. This was the case between the Midland Railway (MR) and the London & North Western Railway (LNWR). The latter had a reputation for being somewhat disreputable and disagreements between the two companies were not unusual.

'Over the hill' in the Derwent Valley the MR line went from Derby to Leeds, and from a junction at Ambergate in 1849 the Manchester, Buxton, Matlock & Midland Junction Railway (MBMMJR) opened its line to Rowsley via Cromford, from where the MR could then have an agreement to jointly run to Manchester. The MR and the Manchester & Birmingham Railway (MBR) were joint promoters, but the MBR was then taken over by the LNWR and therefore became a potential threat to the MR for through running to Manchester.

During 1862 the Midland Railway decided not to take any chances with its precarious relationship with the LNWR and set about constructing another route to Rowsley from a new junction at Duffield, south of Ambergate,

On the line from Wirksworth an unidentified Class 45 diesel with a selection of open wagons, probably filled with stone dust, hence the covers, waits to join the Derby main line at Duffield Junction circa 1967. The semaphore signal on the gantry at the end of the platform on the main line has been cleared for a northbound train. *Neil Ferguson-Lee, Wyvern Rail*

This is Duffield station looking towards Derby, circa 1960, with a rake of empty stone wagons with a guard's van waiting to be taken to Wirksworth. Alongside the platform stands a two-car DMU, built at BR Derby Works after 1955, operating between Derby and Wirksworth. In the background a train is seen pulling away from the main-line platform headed by a Midland 4-4-0. *Neil Ferguson-Lee, Wyvern Rail*

up the Ecclesbourne Valley to Wirksworth and beyond to Rowsley. In the event the LNWR relinquished its interest in the MBMMJR line, leaving the MR to have through running to Manchester. The new line to Rowsley was therefore not required and the line terminated at Wirksworth.

Thus Wirksworth suddenly found itself the terminus of a Midland Railway branch line! The line officially opened for passengers on 1 October 1867 with the first train arriving to an enthusiastic greeting from hundreds of locals – but if relationships between the MR and LNWR had been more amiable, the MR would probably have been reluctant to construct a branch line to Wirksworth. The line was 8 miles 814 yards (13.54km) long from Duffield Junction and 13.2 miles (21.12 km) from Derby, with three intermediate stations.

In 1870 the MR, knowing that it now had running rights through to Manchester, also set wheels in motion to construct an unnecessary three-quarter-mile (1.2km) connection from Wirksworth, up a steep incline to the Cromford & High Peak Railway (C&HPR), possibly for moving mineral traffic onto the MR. There is no evidence whether or how the connection with the C&HPR was made. A section exists today up to the end of the 1 in 30 incline.

The Wirksworth branch brought in coal, general supplies and agricultural materials, but saw increasing outward movement of stone from the numerous local limestone quarries. It appears that five quarries had some form of rail link to Wirksworth station yard, with Dale Quarry being linked by a standard-gauge tunnel under the town. Bailycroft was another quarry with a connecting tunnel, and a narrow-gauge railway. Several other quarries had their own internal narrow-gauge railways that terminated at transfer sidings between the station and the incline.

After the Second World War passengers took to buses, and passenger trains were suspended from 16 June 1947, but mineral trains continued, with stone from Middlepeak Quarry until final

On a very wintery April day in 1953 Wirksworth station hosts the 'High Peak Railtour'. The locomotive, designed by Samuel Johnson, is a Class '2228' 0-4-4T built circa 1897. It was withdrawn in 1955. Note the full stone wagons ready for collection.
Neil Ferguson-Lee, Wyvern Rail

This rare colour photo shows Wirksworth station yard circa 1970, full of activity with wagons being filled with quarried stone from a loading dock in the foreground by lorries of Hoveringham Stone Ltd. The station building has been demolished and the whole operation has been taken over to move stone from the local quarries. The Dust Dock is still in operation and a number of wagons on the former platform side look as though they have been filled with limestone dust and are ready to move. *Neil Ferguson-Lee, Wyvern Rail*

closure in December 1989.

Today, the line now thrives as the heritage Ecclesbourne Valley Railway, with both steam and diesel locomotives on its stock list. The line is fully open from Wirksworth to Platform 3 at Duffield station where connection can be made with the national network from Platforms 1 and 2 on the former Midland Railway main line between Derby and Leeds.

During the 1970s a Class 45 diesel slowly negotiates Wirksworth yard with a rake of stone wagons that it has brought down from quarries a little way up the incline. On the left is the Dust Dock, built in the 1960s where limestone dust from quarries, mainly from those along the Cromford & High Peak Railway, to facilitate closure of the line, could be tipped from lorries directly into railway wagons. *Neil Ferguson-Lee, Wyvern Rail*

This well-turned-out GWR locomotive, Class '5600' 0-6-2T No 5643, was designed by Collett and built at Swindon Works in 1925. It was withdrawn from service in 1963, but saved from being scrapped. Seen here in Wirksworth yard in May 2013, it is getting ready to take out a train for an enthusiasts' photo-shoot.
Neil Ferguson-Lee, Wyvern Rail

This view of Wirksworth station and yard in 2013 still shows the raised loading platform of the old Dust Dock. A new station building has not yet taken shape, but some clean and shining BR Mark 1 coaches are in the platform. On the right by the small platform area is a Class 122 single-coach 'bubble car' unit, No W5506. It was built by the Gloucester Carriage & Wagon Co in 1958. Following the line back to the right, the incline can be clearly seen.

Left: Puffing away in Wirksworth yard is an Andrew Barclay 0-4-0ST locomotive, built in 1947 in Kilmarnock, Works No W2217. Apart from shunting in the yard it carries out duties for loco driving courses.

Right: This photo, taken in 2013, shows the entrance to the tunnel built for standard-gauge rail operation from Wirksworth yard, which went under the town and emerged in Dale Quarry, known locally as 'the big 'ole'! In 1925 it became Wirksworth Quarries and was then taken over by the Tarmac Group and eventually closed in 1968.

Cromford & High Peak Railway

The wild moors and limestone crags of the Derbyshire High Peak district are the home of the once busy mineral railway that struck out from Cromford Wharf on the Cromford Canal to Whaley Bridge on the Peak Forest Canal. Initially a canal was to be constructed to connect these two canals, but the terrain proved that to be an impossible task, so a railway was built instead to carry out the job of canal barges.

This mineral railway was constructed in two sections; the first, of 15½ miles (24.8km) from Cromford Wharf to Hurdlow, opened to traffic on 29 May 1830, and the remaining 17½ miles (28km) from Hurdlow to Whaley Bridge near Buxton in the west opened on 6 July 1831. The high terrain forced several inclined planes to be constructed, four near Cromford and two near Whaley Bridge, which were operated by stationary steam engines; the rest of the line relied on horses for motive power.

By 1833 standard-gauge steam locomotives began to replace the horses, but it took another 30 years before all the horses were replaced. The line operated in total isolation until 21 February 1853, when a three-quarter-mile (1.2km) spur connected it to the Manchester, Buxton, Matlock & Midland Junction Railway (later part of the Midland Railway) at High Peak Junction, Cromford. At Whaley Bridge a similar quarter-mile (0.4km) spur gave access to the Stockport, Disley & Whaley Bridge Railway.

Most of the inclines were double track with haulage ropes and chains that were engaged with the wagons by the 'hanger-on'. His job was essential for the smooth and safe operation of the inclines. The abundance of inclines on a single railway must have been unique. It is interesting to note that Derbyshire County Council had several of its own private-owner, four-plank wagons, which were suitably liveried with its name; it was probably unique for a local authority to own such wagons.

The first incline after Cromford Canal Wharf was at Sheep Pasture, with an inclination of 1 in 9, then 1 in 8 for a distance of 1,320 yards. Before reaching the renowned Middleton Top incline, there was a separate incline down a steep escarpment connecting the Wirksworth goods yard of the Midland Railway; the trackbed was built but the winding engine

One of the 0-4-0ST locomotives was No 47007, built in November 1953 at Horwich Works. Originally of LMS design and built by Kitson, this had extended side tanks. Its last duties were from Rowsley shed and it was withdrawn in December 1963. It is seen here resting between duties at Sheep Pasture Top near High Peak Junction. *Derbyshire County Council*

was not implemented. Along the length of the Cromford & High Peak Railway (C&HPR) there were 19 private sidings into stone quarries and a few other industries, which of course provided the bulk of the traffic. As there were several isolated communities without water supplies, the railway was useful in resolving the problem; a variety of former locomotive tenders full of water were dropped off at suitable locations to provide drinking water as well as water for locomotives.

In 1862 an Act of Parliament permitted a lease to the London & North Western Railway (LNWR), then a further Act in 1887 allowed an amalgamation that ensured development of a line branching to Buxton and a new line from Parsley Hay to Ashbourne; these were completed by June 1894.

A number of steam locomotives were employed over the years, the first being an 0-4-0 built by Robert Stephenson & Co in 1833 and named *Peak*; two years later a 2-2-0 tender loco was supplied by E. Bury, followed in 1842 by an 0-6-0 tender loco built by the Vulcan Foundry.

A motley collection continued to be delivered over the years, including Webb-designed 2-4-0s and 'Crewe Goods' 2-4-0s. The beginning of the 1930s saw delivery of two delightful 0-6-0 tanks, formerly with the North London Railway, which proved to be great favourites on the C&HPR. Three LMS-designed 0-4-0 tank engines with half saddle tanks and conventional side tanks carried out shunting duties at Cromford. At the western end of the line, MR 0-6-0 tender locomotives and a Class 3F worked the Hindlow to Ladmanlow section, with ex-LNWR 0-8-0 and Class 4F 0-6-0 and 8F 2-8-0 tender locos on heavy freight trains. Ex-LMS 2-6-4 tanks saw much of the passenger traffic.

The last service was hauled on 21 April 1967 by an 0-6-0 saddle tank, with the Friden to Parsley Hay section closing in September of that year. The Ashbourne to Buxton line was closed in November 1954. Fortunately Derbyshire County Council acquired the trackbed between Cromford Wharf and Hurdlow and also the Ashbourne to Buxton branch line south of

This J. C. Park-designed North London Railway 0-6-0T locomotive was built at the North London Railway Works, Bow, in December 1899 and withdrawn in 1960. Its last duties were from Rowsley shed. It is now preserved on the Bluebell Railway in West Sussex. *Derbyshire County Council*

Parsley Hay, which were converted into the High Peak Trail and the Tissington Trail respectively.

Today only the Middleton Top engine house remains, which once also had a single-road engine shed. This incline closed in 1963, but fortunately preservationists have restored the machinery to working order.

This view of the Middleton Top engine house dates from 1967. The beam engine became redundant following the closure of the Middleton Incline in 1963. Unfortunately, this severed the line into two sections, hastening the final closure of the line. An unidentified 0-6-0ST sits by the water tank. Note the BMC Riley 1.5 saloon car of the era. *Derbyshire County Council*

There was no mains water up in 'them there 'ills', so it had to be moved by the railway. Apart from housing and commercial use along the line, it was also required to refill locomotives en route. This was achieved by platform wagons with water tanks secured to them. In this picture, taken in 1916, the wagon with man and bicycle on board is ascending Sheep Pasture. *Derbyshire County Council*

This pictures shows a rather isolated Friden yard with virtually no traffic apart from a couple of wagons and an 'Austerity' 0-6-0ST locomotive designed by Riddles for the Ministry of Supply and built by Hunslet in 1944. It was then purchased by the LNER in 1946 and classed as a 'J94'. It was withdrawn in October 1967. *Derbyshire County Council*

This view of Tissington station on the Ashbourne to Buxton branch during November 1954 shows a depleted local freight train idling alongside the platform and in no hurry to move on. The track on the other side was removed that same year. The unidentified locomotive is probably an MR/LMS Fowler Class 3F 0-6-0 tender locomotive.

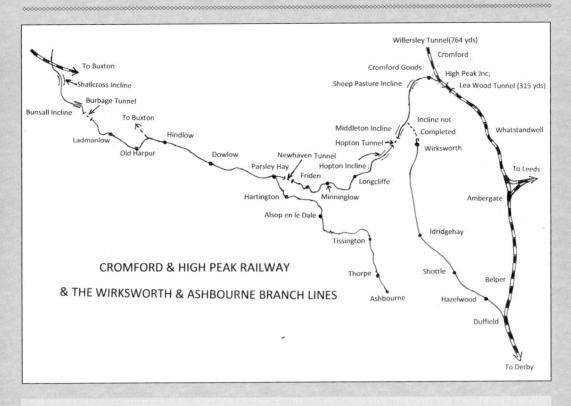

CROMFORD & HIGH PEAK RAILWAY

& THE WIRKSWORTH & ASHBOURNE BRANCH LINES

Yorkshire glass

When Yorkshire is mentioned, it conjures pictures of the beautiful Dales, the North Yorkshire Moors, the City of York and the National Railway Museum, but the county also had some heavy industrial areas like Sheffield, Leeds and Doncaster. It also has a history of glass-making going back to the 17th century, which is depicted on Barnsley's coat of arms, which shows a miner and a glass-blower. Barnsley was also where Hiram Codd, in 1870, invented a unique marble stopper for fizzy drink bottles, where the marble was held against a rubber ring to prevent the fizz from escaping. 'Wallop' was and still is a slang word for beer, so the term 'a load of codswallop' was a disdainful comment about someone having a soft drink. Today people use it as slang for talking rubbish. Back then raw materials of coal and sand for glass-making were sourced locally.

But of course times change and the manufacture of glass and most other commodities has become a highly automated, technical and precise operation, and today there are three particular plants in Barnsley, Doncaster and Goole that use vast quantities of silica sand from Leziate near King's Lynn in Norfolk (see 'Norfolk sand') for manufacturing glass.

Trains leave Leziate three times a day for Yorkshire with around 25 four-wheeled covered hopper wagons of silica sand hauled by GB Railfreight Class 66 locomotives. Leaving King's Lynn the train travels 140 miles (224km) northward through Downham Market, Ely, March, Peterborough, Grantham and Retford to the receiving glassworks. After Retford, Doncaster is next going north, with Barnsley 12 miles (19.2km) west and Goole 16 miles (25.6km) east down the side of the River Humber.

Ardagh Glass UK is one of many facilities of the Ardagh Group, which has plants in 22 countries manufacturing glass and metal products, with its headquarters in Luxembourg. It also includes the household name of Rockware Glass Co of Greenford in Middlesex, which it acquired in 1977.

Ardagh's modern Barnsley plant is accessed by rail via the shortened branch line to the former local colliery at Monk Bretton, which is leased to the company. The hopper wagons are discharged from their underside, between the rails, onto a conveyor system in an undercover shed built for that purpose.

The company's Doncaster facility operates from a former Pilkington Glass factory, another household name, especially in double glazing and motor vehicle window glass. The deliveries of silica sand come into the complex on a short single spur from the Doncaster, Cleethorpes and Grimsby line normally used by South TransPennine Trains. Once inside the perimeter the line splits into two and both tracks enter a shed where the silica sand is discharged, as in Barnsley.

Both the Barnsley and Doncaster plants manufacture bottles of one kind or another for the beer, wine, spirits, alcopop, soft drinks and food industries.

The third facility at Goole is the modern glassworks of Guardian Glass UK Ltd, which specialises in 'float' glass, which is a Pilkington process where molten glass is floated on a bed of molten metal to produce an ultra-flat sheet of glass ideal for conservatories. The plant's range covers just about every type of fine glass that is required in today's world. Delivery of the sand to the plant is by a short, single-track spur just south-west of Goole railway station on the Doncaster-Hull route. The spur runs around the south side of the plant complex and turns north, where the track splits with a short loop line, one into the discharge shed, the other bypassing the shed and rejoining again before the end stop.

GB Railfreight has a contract with Sibelco, the owner of the Norfolk sand quarries, to transport the silica sand to the three glassworks in specially designed top-loading, bottom-discharging Greenbrier 101 6-tonne hopper bogie wagons, built in Poland. The trains are normally hauled by GBRf Class 66 diesel-electric locomotives manufactured by Electro Motive Diesels (EMD) with General Motors (GM) traction engines.

It is an impressive sight as these industrial, streamlined trains of the 21st century snake their way up to their Yorkshire destinations.

Pristine Class 47 diesel-electric No 47843 *Vulcan* gradually pulls some bottom-discharge sand wagons through the covered unloading facility at the Ardagh Glass works at Kirk Sandall, Doncaster, in 2014. It will then take the empty wagons back to Sibelco at Leziate in Norfolk. *Mark Wyard*

Another view of No 47843 pulling the 'WBB Minerals' CovHop wagons through the covered sand-unloading shed. These wagons have since been withdrawn from service and replaced by a more current version manufactured in Poland. *Mark Wyard*

During 2014 Class 47 No 47815 powers towards Kirk Sandall Junction from Norfolk with 34 four-wheeled PA CovHop wagons of sand destined for the Guardian glassworks at Goole. These wagons hold 37 tonnes of sand and were built by W. H. Davis of Langwith Junction for British Industrial Sand. *Mark Wyard*

GBRf have leased from Nacco 41 11A(f) bogie hopper wagons for a five-year contract. These 101.6-tonne wagons are built in Poland and carry 70 tonnes, which is almost double that of the former CovHop wagons. They run in units of 14 with a maximum speed, when empty, of 75mph (121km/h). *Des Hewitt, Ardagh Glass*

Carlisle station

Carlisle, in Cumbria, is a border city between England and Scotland and dates back to Roman times when Hadrian built his frontier wall. As the centuries moved on the city took on a role of influence, no more so than in the development of the railways.

Carlisle station, or Carlisle Citadel as it is known, opened on 10 September 1847, although there were a number of other stations located around the city serving different railway companies. By 1851 it had become the major station and by 1876 the Midland Railway had reached Carlisle with its Settle-Carlisle main line. By this time Citadel station had been enlarged and rebuilt to serve the seven railway companies that used it, the North Eastern, London &

A Class 221 Virgin 'Voyager' is just about to leave for the south. Built by Bombardier Transportation, these trains first saw service in April 2002. New train operator Avanti West Coast have now taken over the franchise

North Western, Midland, Caledonian, North British, Glasgow & South Western and Maryport & Carlisle.

Citadel soon became the frontier hub of the railways. The rail network around the station was complex with routes radiating out in all directions together with engine sheds, carriage sheds and marshalling yards. Since the heady days of steam some lines have closed, facilities to support steam locomotives have disappeared and diesel and electric traction is the norm.

Today Carlisle Citadel is Grade II listed, owned by Network Rail and managed by Avanti West Coast. It has eight platforms serving the West Coast Main Line, Cumbrian Coast line, TransPennine Express, Tyne Valley Line, Settle-Carlisle line and Glasgow South Western line.

Avanti, West Coast provide the regular West Coast Main Line long-distance trains between London Euston and Glasgow Central and Edinburgh Waverley. Carlisle is also a destination for steam-hauled railway excursions travelling up the Settle-Carlisle line and the West Coast Main Line; typical locomotives used are LMS Stanier 4-6-0 Class 5, normally referred to as 'Black Fives'.

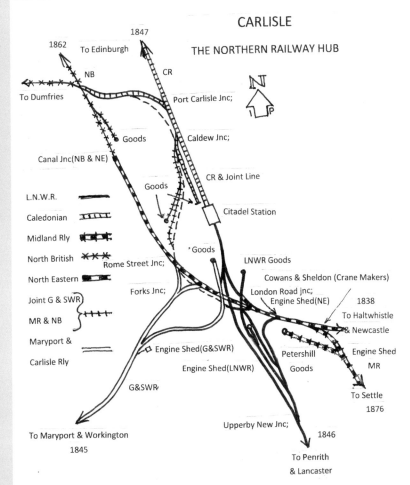

CARLISLE

THE NORTHERN RAILWAY HUB

- 1847
- 1862
- To Edinburgh
- NB
- CR
- To Dumfries
- Port Carlisle Jnc;
- Goods
- Caldew Jnc;
- Canal Jnc(NB & NE)
- CR & Joint Line
- Goods
- L.N.W.R.
- Citadel Station
- Caledonian
- Midland Rly
- North British
- Rome Street Jnc;
- Goods
- North Eastern
- LNWR Goods
- Cowans & Sheldon (Crane Makers)
- Joint G & SWR
- Forks Jnc;
- London Road jnc;
- Engine Shed(NE)
- 1838
- MR & NB
- To Haltwhistle
- & Newcastle
- Maryport &
- Engine Shed(G&SWR)
- Petershill
- Engine Shed
- Carlisle Rly
- Engine Shed(LNWR)
- Goods
- MR
- G&SWR
- To Settle
- 1876
- Upperby New Jnc;
- To Maryport & Workington
- 1845
- 1846
- To Penrith
- & Lancaster

Two Class 37s, Nos 37194 and 37087, with a nuclear flask in tow, are laying over waiting for clearance to Sellafield in Cumbria, where the radioactive fuel rods will be reprocessed.

A preserved LMS Stanier Class 5, famously known as a 'Black Five', built in 1945 at Horwich Works, arrives at Carlisle with 'The Waverley' day tour from Skipton, along the Settle-Carlisle line.

A through train of DB Schenker Class 66s going north from Carlisle is headed by No 66085, in EWS livery, furthest from the camera, then Nos 66030, 66097 (in DB Schenker livery) and 66176 as 'tail end Charlie'. Their destination was unknown.

Northern Rail Class 156 'Super Sprinter' DMU No 156469, built in 1989, is ready to depart from bay Platform 5 for Newcastle along the old Newcastle-Carlisle line through Haltwhistle and Hexham; this is now called the Tyne Valley line.

During 2009 First TransPennine Class 185 DMU No 185133 has just arrived at Carlisle from Glasgow Central, a journey time of around 1 hour 10 minutes. These 'Desiro' units were built in Germany by Siemens.

Carlisle Citadel station was built in 1847 and is Grade II listed. It has eight platforms, is owned by Network Rail and managed by Avanti West Coast

Right: One of the most prolific manufacturers of railway turntables and cranes was Cowans, Sheldon & Co of Carlisle, which exported its products around the world. Here we see a turntable in Bandarawella station yard in Sri Lanka, built in 1890 as No 2006.

Below: Here is a fine example of a complete Cowans, Sheldon steam-operated breakdown train at Dal Josafat, South Africa, in 2001.

Below right: Black Five' No 45305 approaches the summit at Ais Gill on the famous Settle to Carlisle line in typical high bleak countryside.

Haltwhistle and Alston

The Newcastle & Carlisle Railway (N&CR) was opened between 1835 and 1839 and was the first to cross England. The line is still in use and is considered to be relatively unaltered, retaining many of the station buildings, signal boxes and other engineering structures of the N&CR and its successor, the North Eastern Railway (NER), which took over in 1876.

Probably the two most interesting stations on this line are Haltwhistle and Hexham (in Northumberland), both of which have Grade II listed signal boxes painted in the NER livery of

During August 2016 Class 66 No 66733 hauls a rake of steel hopper wagons under Hexham signal box gantry and enters Hexham station on the Tyne Valley line heading towards Haltwhistle and Carlisle. *Adrian Booth*

Right: A sad-looking Alston station is seen in 1973 with the canopy, the goods shed and sidings all removed. Steam has now been replaced by Class 101 DMUs on the countdown to closure in May 1976.
John Alsop collection

Below right This is the view of Haltwhistle station and signal box today, looking towards Carlisle. The station was opened in 1838 as part of the Newcastle & Carlisle Railway. The signal box was built in 1901 and closed in 1993. Haltwhistle was the junction and goods yard for the Alston line, but this photo shows all that now remains.

Bottom right: This splendid water tower, built in 1861 by Wylie of Newcastle, still occupies the end of Haltwhistle's eastbound platform, although without any functional use.

cream and burgundy. Haltwhistle box was built with 85 levers by the NER and opened in 1901, and Hexham in 1896. Alas, there are no semaphore signals to complete these nostalgic scenes today apart from one at the end of Hexham platform used for a short siding running under the signal gantry.

Around 1851 Haltwhistle found itself a junction station and became known as 'Haltwhistle change for Alston' when a 13½-mile (21.6km) branch line opened in stages to Alston, a small market town in the North Pennines. At Haltwhistle the branch line that had its own side of an island platform. The station area included a turntable, goods shed, cattle docks and sidings and also boasted a very handsome water tank built in 1861.

STATION AND BRIDGES - HALTWHISTLE.

Above: This excellent photo shows the layout of Haltwhistle Junction station in the days of steam. The signal box and footbridge can be seen at the end of the island platform with the Alston branch using the right-hand platform face. The line swept round to the right and across the bridge over the River South Tyne. LNER Class 'Q6' 0-8-0 No 2259 can be seen with a mixed freight train. *John Alsop collection*

Right: Leaving Haltwhistle Junction the line climbed and crossed the River South Tyne a second time by Lambley Viaduct, which was 850 feet (260 metres) long and stood about 108 feet (33 metres) above the river. A sharp left curve at the Alston end took the line into Lambley station, which is now a private house. *John Alsop collection*

LAMBLEY VIADUCT.

The Alston line

The Alston line opened fully in 1852, and from its island platform at Haltwhistle it followed a bend in the River South Tyne a short distance before curving right and crossing the river on the Alston Arches Viaduct. In 1919 a colliery was opened at Plenmeller, not far from the viaduct, so a basic timber halt was built to serve colliery workmen only. The colliery had its own small tramway and transfer sidings connected to the branch line. The halt closed in 1932 but reopened during the Second World War to serve the Ministry of Supply until 1946.

The line roughly follows the River South Tyne upstream and crosses it again at Lambley Viaduct, an elegant piece of architecture with nine arches looming 120 feet (36.6 metres) above the river. Once across the viaduct the line converged with the freight line from Lambley Fell and Brampton, then entered Lambley station. The only other station of note was Slaggyford, serving a small village with basic amenities.

Finally the line reached its terminus at Alston, an attractive market town 1,000 feet (304.8 metres) above sea level in the Cumbrian North Pennines at the confluence of the Rivers South Tyne and Nent. The station consisted of a main platform with canopy, turntable, engine shed, goods shed and coal yard.

However, in common with many small struggling branch lines of the 1960s, goods

Right: Alston station in 2015 is now part of the South Tynedale narrow-gauge railway. This view is looking in the Haltwhistle direction. The station is now in good condition with a level crossing and relocated signal box at the end of the platform.

Below right: One of the South Tynedale's locomotives is *Naklo,* an 0-6-0 built in Poland in 1957, which worked in the Naklo sugar factory. It arrived at Alston in 1988 and was rebuilt, which included an improved tender to carry more coal and water. It is seen here running round at Alston after having just arrived with a busy train.

services were withdrawn, intermediate stations became unstaffed and steam-hauled trains were replaced with Class 101 DMUs. By that time there was only one train on the line and the signalling became redundant apart from at the junction at Haltwhistle. Although the line was marked for closure under the Beeching plan, it managed to linger on, due to the lack of an all-weather road to Alston. The line was officially closed on 3 May 1976.

The South Tynedale Railway

During 1973, prior to BR's closure of the branch line, the South Tynedale Railway Company and the South Tynedale Railway Preservation Society (STRPS) fought to keep the line open, but failed in that attempt.

Reprieve of a different kind came to the closed branch line in 1977 when the reconstituted STRPS took the decision to buy a length of trackbed from BR to construct a 2-foot (610mm) narrow-gauge line northwards from Alston, back towards Haltwhistle. The first mile was opened on 30 July 1983 and extensions have continued, the line currently terminating at Slaggyford some 5 miles (8km) from Alston. Work is continuing to take the line towards Lambley. It is most unlikely that the line will ever reach Haltwhistle in the near future, as that town's bypass necessitated the removal of the railway embankment leading from the Alston Arches Viaduct over the River South Tyne.

Alston station has been carefully restored and has now had a second platform constructed with a canopy over both. The original signal box was removed at the time of closure and has now been replaced by the box from the former North Eastern Railway's Ainderby to Redmire branch in North Yorkshire, which closed in 1954.

Motive power is a mixture of steam and diesel locomotives with some fine coaches, some built locally and others from Sierra Leone (originally built by the Gloucester Railway Carriage & Wagon Co) and Romania.

The Quintinshill railway disaster

The Quintinshill accident of 22 May 1915, on the Anglo-Scottish border, is without doubt Britain's worst rail disaster and has since gained the notoriety of being surrounded by operational failures, secrets and conspiracies to suppress the whole truth being told at that time. Many books, journals and newspaper articles have been written, putting forward their views, and each time maybe adding a little more to the underlying causes of the accident.

During May 1915 the First World War was in full swing and all the railway companies in the UK were being used to transport goods, armaments and service personnel to strategic ports for shipment to France and onward

Top to bottom: Caledonian 'Cardean' Class 4-6-0 locomotive No 907 was heading the down slow passenger train that was sitting facing the oncoming troop train on the up line. Here is an example of the class, No 903 *Cardean*. These locomotives were designed by John F. McIntosh and built at the company's St Rollox Works in 1906.

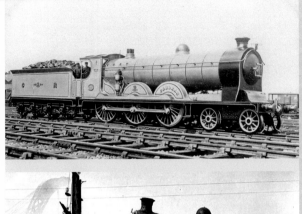

The second London to Glasgow express that collided with the debris was doubled-headed, with Caledonian Class '721' 4-4-0 No 140 at the front. It was built at the Caledonian's St Rollox Works in 1896 and is seen here after the collision resting against the tender of the troop train's Class '139' No 121, which it propelled forward with great force.

After the accident survivors were taken into the fields on either side of the railway line to receive first aid and to await being moved to various hospitals, which were few and far between. The dead were taken to barns used as makeshift mortuaries.

This is the London to Glasgow express's sleeping car, after the second collision, completely enveloped in smoke and flames. It should be borne in mind that the rolling stock of the day was mainly wood and was quick to ignite.

transportation to the front lines. At the same time, long-distance passenger traffic on the West Coast Main Line from London Euston to Glasgow was still a priority for the two competing companies, the London & North Western and Caledonian railways, and the Great Northern and North British railways. Both ran prestigious overnight sleepers with all the 'mod cons' of the day. The bad news was that the war was worsening, with daily reports of our failures at Gallipoli (Turkey), disasters in France, a gross shortage of shells, and the sinking of the Cunard liner RMS *Lusitania* by a German U-boat. Because of the mounting losses the War Office was under severe attack from all sides within the UK, but none of this seemed to count for anything with the profit-minded railway companies who wanted their prestigious trains to arrive on time at their destinations.

The whys and wherefores of the causes of the accident are too numerous and complex to state here, but the following describes briefly what happened on that

Right top to bottom: This picture shows the sleeping car after the fire, which had been brought under control once the *Top to bottom:* Carlisle Fire Brigade arrived, but it was well over an hour before they did so and little could be done, as the fires were well out of control by that time.

Located on the side of the bridge parapet crossing the West Coast Main Line is this poignant 2009 memorial plaque in memory of the men of the 7th Royal Scots, 'Leith's Own', who died in the Quintinshill disaster, with words by Denis Muir.

A rake of ballast wagons top-and-tailed by two Class 66s (No 66520 seen here at the rear) heads towards Gretna and Carlisle. The train is just passing the southbound loop line, and the space where Quintinshill signal box once stood can be seen on the left about half way down the loop.

An SB Rail Plasser Theurer tamping machine makes its way into the southbound loop to allow a passenger train to pass at speed towards Carlisle.

fateful Saturday morning in May.

Because of the situation in Gallipoli a train carrying 500 Scottish soldiers was coming south on the Caledonian's main up line, at high speed, heading for Liverpool Docks for their transfer to the Gallipoli beaches, when it collided with a stationary local passenger train that was facing it at Quintinshill, having been shunted onto the up line to let a down express pass. A minute later the Glasgow-bound express from London collided with the wreckage that was spread across the down line. The result was 230 dead and another 247 injured.

Quintinshill was an isolated spot and its signal box overlooked the up and down main lines, each of which had a loop line with head shunts and a reverse crossover between the two main lines. It was responsible for the section between Gretna Junction to the south and Kirkpatrick to the north.

It was, and still is, common practice for slow-moving freight and passenger traffic to be temporarily parked on outer loops to allow faster traffic to speed through, and this certainly was the case at Quintinshill, especially with up to 40% extra wartime traffic.

On this occasion at about 6.00am the

signalman, George Meakins, parked an empty coal train in the up loop ready for the fast, and already late, troop train to pass. Meakins should have finished his shift at 6.00am, but it appears that his replacement and friend, James Tinsley, was often late, having hitched a lift on the slow passenger train from Carlisle to Beattock that would be stopped at Quintinshill by Meakins. That was the case on that fateful morning.

At 6.30am, as there was already a coal train in the down loop, Meakins took the decision to reverse the Carlisle-Beattock passenger train across to the up line, facing the oncoming troop train. This freed the down line to allow two express passenger trains from London to pass at speed. The first passed and went on its way. Both signalmen were now in the box together with Tinsley writing the train movements into the Train Register Book from 6.00am that Meakins had written on a scrap of paper for him. If Meakins had written them in the book it would have been seen in Meakins's handwriting and not Tinsley's.

At 6.42am the up troop train was offered to Quintinshill and accepted, but it appears that Tinsley was unaware that the slow passenger train he had alighted from was still on up line and Meakins seemingly had not realised the disastrous implications of his acceptance of the troop train. He had not contacted the Kirkpatrick signalman to tell him that the slow passenger train was facing the troop train on the up line and had not used the signal lever locking collar over the handle; had he done so, it would have prevented the signal for the up line from clearing the path to Quintinshill, possibly avoiding the accident.

At 6.50am the troop train hurtled at speed into the local passenger train and a few seconds later the second double-headed express passenger train from London hit the wreckage at speed. The result was almost total disintegration of the front carriages of all trains, except the troop train, which consisted of very old wooden carriages. Those that were not smashed to pieces quickly caught fire owing to gas containers under the flooring for gas lighting, causing many of the injured soldiers to burn to death.

This is not the place to conduct an inquest, but it seems that sloppy practices were allowed to continue between station masters, signalmen (Tinsley claimed to be ill), line inspectors and probably with the knowledge of the top brass of the Caledonian Railway, who wanted their superior express trains to be the best and on time at any cost. The two signalmen were found guilty of culpable homicide (manslaughter) and imprisoned, after which they were reemployed by the Caledonian Railway! Also, HM Government obviously wanted this nasty episode to be as low-key as possible because of all the other problems arising from the war at that time.

A TransPennine Express service travels at speed under the road bridge and past the notorious Quintinshill disaster spot towards Carlisle from Edinburgh. The train consists of two four-car Class 350 EMUs, built by Siemens in 2005. I doubt that any passengers on the many trains that fly past this spot every day know what took place on 22 May 1915.

The Caledonian Railway in all its blue splendour: the 'River' Class 4-6-0s, built in 1915 for the Highland Railway, were found to be too heavy, so were sold to the Caledonian!

HM Explosives Plant, Gretna

As the First World War proceeded it was obvious that not enough shells were being produced to meet the increasing demands of the armies in France, so something more drastic had to be done to increase production of cordite, a mixture of nitro-glycerine and nitro-cellulose. To overcome the shortage the decision was made to construct a completely new site for the purpose. The site eventually chosen was in the Scottish county of Dumfriesshire, along the Solway Firth. It was agricultural land, fairly flat and accessible by the three Scottish railway systems of the Glasgow & South Western, which ran from Carlisle to Glasgow via Dumfries, the Caledonian, running from Carlisle to Glasgow via Lockerbie (and also from Lockerbie over the Annan Viaduct across the Solway into Cumbria), and the North British, running from Carlisle via Longtown to Edinburgh. Construction materials for the site were brought in via these various lines, and temporary sidings laid.

The munitions girls wield their pick-axes to break up the great pile of crystalline nitrate to fill up the narrow-gauge wagons, in which it will be transported to another safe location to be turned into nitric acid, a core ingredient in the manufacture of cordite. *The Devil's Porridge Museum*

The factory was constructed over a large area and consisted of four self-contained sections, isolated from each other for safety reasons, stretching over 11 miles (17.6km) and designed

Top to bottom: The narrow-gauge electric locomotives were battery-powered for safety reasons and were used to transport the cordite over the longer distances between sites. This is loco No 5 with a headlamp on the roof, as cordite production was continuous for 24 hours, seven days a week.

This photo shows the workers arriving back at the Gretna Township after their night shift at Mossband Site 2. The factory had its own police force of both men and especially women constables, as a majority of workers were women. The police can be seen here keeping an eye on proceedings. *The Devil's Porridge Museum*

This is one of the 0-6-0 fireless locomotives used at the factory, where safety was required in areas where there was a high risk of explosion. It was built by Andrew Barclay & Co of Kilmarnock and delivered to the Gretna factory in 1917. After the war it was sold to the CEGB and named *Sir James*. It is now on permanent display outside The Devil's Porridge Museum in Eastriggs. *The Devil's Porridge Museum*

Seen here is *Sir James* in working mode with its new owner at Brimsdown Generating Station (CEGB) in London around 1925. It was later transferred to Fleetwood Power Station and in 1975 was moved to the Lakeside Railway at Haverthwaite on the edge of the Lake District National Park. It reached its final resting place at Gretna in 2015.

to receive raw materials at Dornock station to the west. After all the phases of manufacture were completed the cordite was taken away by the North British Railway from the exchange sidings at Longtown to Carlisle, then onward to the various munitions factories for packing into shells, etc.

Extra temporary stations were constructed on the main line at Dornock and Gretna by the Glasgow & South Western Railway for the workers coming from Dumfries, Annan, Lockerbie, Penrith and Carlisle. Around 15,000 workers also lived in two purpose-built townships – Gretna Township and Dornock – at each end of this giant complex, so all workers could board a train on the Ministry of Munitions own internal network to a station very near their place of work.

Internal network
Inside the secure factory area the Ministry of Munitions constructed its own internal railway with both standard-gauge and narrow-gauge networks.

Right: The Devil's Porridge Museum was founded in 1997 at Eastriggs and displays all aspects of the manufacture of cordite during the First World War; it also covers the story of the Quintinshill railway disaster where at least 229 soldiers and civilians lost their lives.
The Devil's Porridge Museum

Below: This diagram shows the western end of Site 3 at Dornock where the initial stages of cordite production took place. The site was around 2½ miles (4km) across from east to west and 1½ miles (2.4km) long going down towards the Solway Firth. The extent and complexity of the internal rail network can be seen, with Wylies Platform to the north to convey workers and goods between the four sites.
The Devil's Porridge Museum

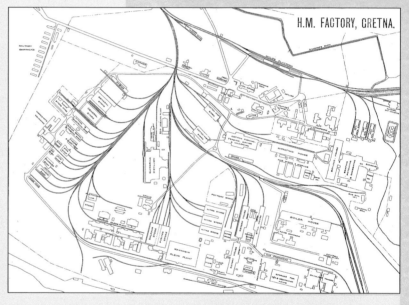

The standard-gauge network had 40½ miles (64.8km) of track, 36½ miles (58.4km) of sidings, and 537 points and crossings. This internal network connected the four sites for transporting both raw materials and employees with several stations conveniently situated near the working areas. The line ran west to east from Dornock to Gretna with a loop running around Site 3 (Eastriggs) where the volatile cordite paste was mixed. On one occasion Sir Arthur Conan Doyle visited the site and named the nasty brew 'Devil's Porridge'.

The standard-gauge network was controlled by 24 signal boxes containing a total of 496 levers activating 281 signals supplied by Tyer & Co. The track sections, some double, were controlled by Tyer's block signalling instruments and the single-track sections by that company's tablet instruments.

The total number of standard-gauge steam locomotives eventually increased to 38, but little is known about them. By 1916 the Ministry of Munitions had ordered and received 11 fireless 0-4-0T locomotives from Andrew Barclay in Kilmarnock, which were able to transport materials, free of dangerous sparks, to the more sensitive, volatile areas. A further six more powerful 0-6-0T locomotives were received from Andrew Barclay in 1917 to transport heavier and longer trains. Fireless locomotives did not require a fire and did not develop their own steam. In this particular case charging stations were conveniently placed around the munitions site where the fireless locomotive would be 'plugged in' via an armoured flexible cable, transferring steam from the charging station's high-pressure boiler to the loco. Charging was complete when the pressure was at 160lb; the loco could then carry on working until the pressure dropped to about 20lb.

The narrow-gauge network consisted of 49 miles (78km) of 2-foot (610mm) track and 10 narrow-gauge locomotives, some of which were electrically powered by battery and looked like something from the fairground! They were used for moving supplies into the factory buildings and removing waste material from sites when required, and to take the cordite paste in special wagons from Site 3 (Eastriggs) to Site 2 (Mossband), a distance of 5 miles (8km). Other narrow-gauge locomotives are assumed to have been petrol-powered. Many small wagons were pushed by both the male and female workers between the manufacturing units both day and night and in all weathers. Apart from the above, very little is known about the narrow-gauge network.

Closure

At its peak the site was producing 800 tons of cordite per week and employed 11,576 women and 5,066 men, a total of 16,642 employees. At the end of the First World War manufacturing ceased and the plant closed completely with most of the sites quickly demolished.

Although Site 4 at Gretna was sold off and returned to agricultural land, the other sites remained the property of the MOD, with Site 2 at Mossband becoming Central Ammunition Depot (CAD) Longtown; after the Second World War it was designated Base Ammunition Depot (BAD). Site 3 at Eastriggs became a sub depot. Eventually, Longtown was known as Defence, Storage and Distribution Agency (DSDA) with its own internal network of narrow-gauge and standard-gauge tracks with connection to the national network. All sites are now closed.

On 15 June 1955 ex-North British Railway Class 'J37' No 64582 with a rake of 15 private-owner 'LGW' bulk grain vans passes Morningside Road on the Edinburgh-Dumbarton line, en route from Leith South to either Georgie or Cameron Bridge Distillery. Cameron Bridge is about 15 miles (24km) north of Edinburgh.
Stuart Sellar collection

Whisky distilleries and their railways

Whenever Scotland is mentioned it seems natural to think about whisky, or 'liquid gold' as it is lovingly called, but why should it be made in the Highlands?

Apart from barley and malt, the most important ingredient is a plentiful supply of soft pure water from sparkling clean burns, which is plentiful in the Speyside area in particular. In early days malt whisky distilleries purchased locally grown barley and each distillery had a malthouse with the distinctive oriental style of pagoda roof to the kilns, an attractive feature that is preserved to this day.

Whisky distilleries could be found across many parts of Scotland, including the Western Isles, but were mostly concentrated on the east side around the River Spey area, their products being commonly known as Speyside whiskies.

Many whisky distilleries were sited so that they had their own railway sidings via a

Right: At Knockando a 36-gallon (164-litre) whisky barrel of W. & G. Gilbey's 1960 blend is loaded onto a 13-ton steel wagon after leaving the distillery on 2 November 1966. Knockando is by the River Spey in Moray, Speyside. An unidentified Birmingham Carriage & Wagon Co Type 2 diesel-electric locomotive, introduced in 1958 for the Scottish Region of BR, stands by. *Aberdeen Journals*

Below left: Muir of Ord is south of Dingwall about 5½ miles (8.8km) west of Inverness, and seen there are bulk grain hopper wagons waiting for their onward travel. *Distillers Company*

Below right: An Aberfeldy branch line train headed by an ex-Caledonian Railway 0-4-0 tank locomotive puffs along with a single coach past the siding of the Aberfeldy Distillery, a short distance from the town that sits by the River Tay in the burgh of Perth and Kinross. *Diagio*

spur from a main line. These became essential with increased demands on production from both home and abroad, and the grain growers from the premier growing areas in the eastern counties of England responded with larger malthouse complexes; most were also connected to the national railway network. Both distilleries and maltings usually owned their own small shunters to move wagons around their yards. They were mainly 0-4-0 steam tank locomotives, which in Scotland were affectionately called 'Pugs', meaning ugly!

During the end of the 1800s many small railways were amalgamated into one of several larger companies, the Great North of Scotland (GNSR), the Highland (HR), the Caledonian (CR), the North British (NBR) and the Glasgow & South Western (G&SWR). Then as a result of the 1921 Railways Act, almost all railway companies were 'grouped' into one of four large organisations in 1923: the G&SWR, HR and CR became part of the London Midland & Scottish Railway (LMS), with the GNSR and NBR forming part of the London & North Eastern Railway (LNER). When the railways were nationalised in 1948, the entire Scottish network became part of the Scottish Region of British Railways.

During the steam age, up to the 1960s, wooden four-wheeled vans and open wagons

At Ballindalloch station, Banffshire, in October 1961 trucks are being shunted to form a 'whisky train' of around 50 wagons to be transported to Glasgow, where there are bonded warehouses and blending facilities. This train ran twice a week until closure of the line in 1967. *Diagio*

were used to transport the raw materials in and the casks of whisky out. Gradually more specialised steel wagons with hopper discharge were used to take the barley and malt up to Scotland. They were painted blue and advertised the whisky brands on their sides. Over the years these became larger-capacity and longer bogie wagons.

As far as the finished product is concerned, the whisky has to be bottled, but it is a legal requirement that it must mature in casks for at least three years before being sold. With whiskies being blended in the Glasgow area, Leith and Perth, the railways transported the full casks of whisky from the distilleries to be bottled. The railways also transported vast volumes to several ports, especially Liverpool, Manchester and Southampton, for export to foreign climes.

Apart from the railways handling full casks, they also handled empty ones, as well as stripped-down casks imported from the USA that were reassembled at cooperages for reuse by the distilleries.

However, like most businesses that relied on British Railways for the delivery of raw materials or to transport the finished products away, the 1960s began to see the end of an era with the closure of unprofitable railway lines and the increase in road transport that was only too eager to take business from the railways.

This 1970s aerial view shows Chivas Brothers' Longmorn Distillery on Speyside, which started in 1894. Note the line coming into the distillery with a white covered van in the siding, three coal wagons near the boiler house, and neatly stacked barrels in the yard. To the left is the removed private branch line to Glenlossie Distillery, seen in the right background of the picture. *Chivas Brothers*

The Scottish distilleries were not exempt and today the railways serving them have completely disappeared.

Fortunately, Scottish whisky continues to be a very popular tipple worldwide, and long may that last!

Top: This 0-6-0 DM No 1446 was built by English Electric in 1967 at its Vulcan Foundry, Newton-le-Willows in Lancashire, and delivered to Seaham Harbour Dock Co. It was then sold on to Scottish Grain Distillers for use at Cameron Bridge Distillery. In 1998 it was outshopped by United Distillers & Vintners in the company's corporate red and yellow livery, and started work at Dufftown on 15 March 2000. This photo was taken in April 2007.

Above: A Barclay & Sons 0-4-0 'Puggie' saddle tank is seen here on display at Aberfeldy Distillery, Perthshire, in May 2008, although its working life was at the Dailuaine Distillery at Carron, some 60 miles (96km) south of Aberfeldy.

Above: This Stromness Distillery poster of 1905 depicts a Highland Railway porter on the Thurso to Wick line, which features the most northerly stations and whisky distillery.

Right: This is Towiemore Distillery near Keith, with a GNSR 4-4-0 arriving on a pick-up goods train to drop off coal wagons and pick up loaded covered vans containing whisky.

Opposite page top: Aultmore Distillery was served by the Highland Railway branch line from Keith to Portessie on the coast; the distillery is still in production today.

West Highland Railway

It goes without saying that the West Highland Line is probably one of the most spectacular and interesting railway journeys one can expect to experience. The trip can be taken by regular ScotRail trains from Glasgow and also by a private steam-hauled train known as the 'Jacobite' between Fort William and Mallaig at certain times, but requires to be pre-booked.

The line runs north from Glasgow Queen Street station to Fort William, where there is an extension to Mallaig on the west coast. Part of the North British Railway, it opened in its entirety in 1901.

Leaving Glasgow Queen Street station the line strikes out north-west along the north bank of the River Clyde to the attractive riverside town of Helensburgh, then north on to Garelochhead. The line then continues north following the east bank of Loch Long to the small town of Tarbet, situated on a narrow stretch of land between the top of Loch Long and Loch Lomond. Continuing on, the line follows the west bank of Loch Lomond, through Glen Falloch to Crianlarich, where the former Caledonian Railway line branches off to Oban. Opened in 1880, this Caledonian line ran from Glasgow to Callander, then across to Crianlarich and on to Oban.

Continuing northwards on the West Highland line the journey takes the traveller to Bridge of Orchy and through the wild countryside to Rannoch Moor station, comprising a single island

On a grey day the 'Jacobite' has just arrived at Mallaig station. The short platform length means that passengers in the rear coaches have to walk through the train to alight.

The Caledonian Sleeper is seen here in 2015 in a siding at Fort William station with Class 67 No 67011 in EWS livery at the helm. The coaches have been in service for some 30 years and have now been replaced by 75 new carriages built in Spain by CAF (Construcciones Auxiliar de Ferrocarriles).

After leaving Fort William the Mallaig line branches west and crosses Thomas Telford's Banavie swing bridge over the Caledonian Canal. The signal box can be seen on the left of the picture.

This is the classic shot of 'The Jacobite' as 'Black Five' No 45407 slowly hauls the train across Robert McAlpine's Glenfinnan Viaduct, clearly showing its curvature and many arches.

platform and a nearby small hotel. Leaving the station the line crosses a steel truss viaduct and winds its way up into the hills.

At Tulloch station at the north end of Loch Treig the line turns westwards through Spean Bridge to Fort William, located at the apex of Loch Linnhe and Loch Eil and a major town in that part of Scotland, lying at the foot of the famous Ben Nevis range. From Spean Bridge a line used to run north to Fort Augustus.

The West Highland Line extension branches away to the west towards Mallaig, crossing a swing bridge over the Caledonian Canal, a masterpiece of engineering built by Scottish engineer Thomas Telford, connecting the Moray Firth in the north to Loch Linnhe in the south. It uses 29 locks to connect lochs through the Great Glen, including the infamous Loch Ness of 'monster' fame.

Having left Loch Eil the train passes over the magnificent curved Glenfinnan Viaduct at the head of Loch Shiel. Built by Robert McAlpine (known as 'Concrete Bob'), it was first unreinforced concrete viaduct – and a wonderful job he made of it! The train then immediately runs into Glenfinnan station and the views are worth waiting for, as the statue of 'Bonnie Prince Charlie' can be seen looking out to sea, commemorating his place of arrival and departure in his bid to rule Scotland. He hoped and failed to restore Catholicism to Scotland and England; known as the Jacobite cause, it gives its name to the private tourist train, the 'Jacobite'.

The line continues west to Lochailort, around the Arisaig peninsula and up to the terminus at Mallaig. The town was founded in the 1840s and its main industry is fishing, especially herring. A ferry runs from the harbour to Armadale at the southern end of the Isle of Skye. The distance from Glasgow to Fort William is 123 miles (197km) and another 41 miles (66km) to Mallaig, giving a total of 164 miles (262km).

Above: The splendid view from Glenfinnan Viaduct looks down the waters of Loch Shiel with the statue of Jacobite Prince Charlie on top of the column signifying where he landed and also where he fled these shores.

Right: At Fort William station 'The Jacobite' train is hauled by Class 5 ('Black Five') 4-6-0 No 45407 *The Lancashire Fusilier.* Designed by William Stanier for the LMS and built in 1935, this example was withdrawn from BR service in 1968.

Index